A WORLD BANK COUNTRY STUDY

Bangladesh

Financial Accountability for Good Governance

The World Bank
Washington, D.C.

Contents

Abstract

This document assesses the quality of financial accountability and transparency in Bangladesh and makes recommendations for improvement. With respect to *public* funds, it compares the financial management standards and practices of agencies using such funds against an international or 'best practice' standard, and also the standards and practices of the external 'oversight' agencies - nine Audit Directorates of the Comptroller and Auditor General's Office, parliamentary committees concerned with public expenditure, donor agencies, and the media. It assesses what it would take to qualify the country for programmatic or sector lending in replacement of all individual project lending. With respect to *private* funds in the hands of companies, commercial banks, insurance companies and non-government organizations, it examines the regulatory activities of the Registrar of Joint Stock Companies, the Securities and Exchange Commission, the two Stock Exchanges, Bangladesh Bank, NGO Affairs Bureau and the accounting and auditing profession that serves both public and private sectors.

Preface

This Country Financial Accountability Assessment was conducted by the World Bank's South Asia Region and the UNDP Program for Accountability and Transparency, with participation from officers in the Ministry of Finance, Comptroller & Auditor General's Office, Ministry of Local Government, Institute of Chartered Accountants of Bangladesh, Parliamentary Financial and Ministerial Oversight Committees and other national stakeholders.

The process started with preparation of papers by local consultants in selected areas:

- Parliamentary control of public expenditures.

- Accountancy profession and education.

- Public sector auditing.

- Budgeting, accounting, reporting and internal control.

- Local government financial management.

National authorities discussed leading issues in workshops for each of the first four areas and responded to the structured questionnaires of the CFAA (World Bank, 1999c - the revised CFAA Part I procedure) and UNDP 2000 (the revised CONTACT). The questionnaires are not sub-divided by level of government and were answered mainly in terms of the central government ministries/divisions. This information was supplemented from local consultants' studies, interviews with officers in representative units, and other sources.

An International Conference on Improving Oversight Functions: Challenges in the New Millennium was held in Dhaka, September 10-12, 2000 with top-level political and civil service participants and inputs from 18 countries. The Conference covered parliamentary control of finance, public audit and the private accounting and auditing profession. Recommendations of the Conference have been included in this CFAA.

◆Acknowledgments

This assessment has been prepared by a task team led by M. Mozammal Hoque and P.K. Subramanian from the World Bank and Fred Schenkelaars and Zahurul Alam from UNDP. Kapil Kapoor was the overall Team Leader for the task. Anthony Bennett worked as the principal consultant. The other members of the team were Shamsuddin Ahmad, Suraiya Zannath, Zafrul Islam, Mohammed Sayeed and Osman Ghani who made useful contributions. The assessment is based on five sectoral studies carried out on Parliamentary Control of Public Expenditure, Public Sector Auditing, Accountancy Profession and Education, Public Sector Budgeting, Accounting and Internal Control, and Financial Accountability in Local Government Institutions. These were carried out by five local consultants and an international consultant.

The review benefited from a number of workshops and also an international conference on "Improving Oversight Functions", organized by the C&AG under the project Strengthening of C&AG Office (STAG). The conference and workshops had participation from Parliamentarians from home and abroad, Controllers and Auditors General from various countries, senior government officials, public and private sector accountants and auditors, leaders of business, NGO representatives and members of civil society. We sincerely acknowledge the contributions made by Syed Yusuf Hossain and Sajedul Karim in organizing the conference.

John Hegarty, Peter Dean, David Shand and Piyush Desai acted as peer reviewers for the study. In addition, useful comments were received from John Fitzsimon, Joe Pernia, Vinod Sahgal, Marc Heitner, Rajesh Dayal and Magdy Soliman.

Funds for the assessment was provided by the World Bank and UNDP. Sincere words of thanks go to the German Government and Government of the Netherlands who made this CFAA possible by generously providing funds to UNDP's Programme for Accountability and Transparency, a partner with the World Bank in this endeavor. UNDP provided the funds for the International Conference through the STAG Project. Pauline Tamesis, Shahadat Hossain Russell, Tanjina Rahman, Hasib Ehsan Chowdhury, Joyce Mormita Das and Mehar Akhter Khan provided very useful assistance.

Abbreviations

ADB	Asian Development Bank
ADP	Annual Development Program
ASIRP	Agricultural Services Innovation and Reform Project
BAS	Bangladesh Accounting Standard
BCS	Bangladesh Civil Service
BIM	Bangladesh Institute of Management
BSA	Bangladesh Standards of Auditing
BTTB	Bangladesh Telegraph and Telephone Board
C&AG	Comptroller and Auditor General
CA	Chartered Accountant
CAO	Chief Accounting Officer
CC	City Corporation
CEO	Chief Executive Officer
CFAA	Country Financial Accountability Assessment
CGA	Controller General of Accounts
CONTACT	Country Assessment of Accountability And Transparency
DAO	District Accounts Officer
DESA	Dhaka Electricity Supply Authority
DfID	Department for International Development (UK)
DG	Director-General
DMFAS	Debt Management and Financial Analysis System
ERD	Economic Relations Division, Ministry of Finance
ESTEEM	Effective Schools Through Enhanced Education Management (project)
FIMA	Financial Management Academy (formerly Audit and Accounts Training Academy)
FM	Financial Management
FY	Financial Year. The Government of Bangladesh (central and local) has a Financial year July 1 to June 30. FY00 means the year July 1, 1999 – June 30, 2000. Banks use the calendar year, January 1 – December 31
GDP	Gross Domestic Product
GFR	General Financial Rules
GFS	Government Finance Statistics (IMF system)
GOB	Government of Bangladesh
IAS	International Accounting Standards
ICAB	Institute of Chartered Accountants of Bangladesh
ICMAB	Institute of Management Accountants of Bangladesh
IFAC	International Federation of Accountants
IMED	Implementation, Monitoring and Evaluation Division, Ministry of Planning
IMF	International Monetary Fund
INTOSAI	International Organization of Supreme Audit Institutions
IPSAS	International Public Sector Accounting Standards (issued by IFAC)
IRD	Internal Revenue Division, Ministry of Finance
ISA	International Standards of Auditing
LGI	Local Government Institution
MAAB	Management Accounting, Auditing and Budgeting (FIMA course)
MBA	Master's Degree in Business Administration
MIS	Management Information System
MLGRDC	Ministry of Local Government, Rural Development and Cooperatives

MOE	Ministry of Education
NCB	Nationalized Commercial Bank
NFPE	Non-Financial Public Enterprise
NGO	Non-Government Organization
NILG	National Institute of Local Government
O&M	Operations and Maintenance
OECD	Organisation for Economic Co-operation and Development
PAC	Standing Committee on Public Accounts
PAO	Principal Accounting Officer (secretary of a ministry or division)
PARC	Public Administration Reforms Commission
PATC	Public Administration Training Centre
PC	Parliamentary Committee
PCR	Project Completion Report
PDB	Power Development Board
PEC	Standing Committee on Estimates
PUC	Standing Committee on Public Undertakings
PWD	Public Works Department
RAO	Regional Accounts Officer
RIBEC	Reforms in Budgeting and Expenditure Control (DfID-assisted project)
RIGA	Reforms in Government Auditing (DfID-assisted project)
SAS	Subordinate Accounts Service
SCM	Standing Committees on the Ministries (Parliament)
SCE	Securities and Exchange Commission
SD	Statistics Division, Ministry of Planning
SHAPLA	Strengthening Health and Population for the Less Advantaged (DfID-assisted project)
STAG	Strengthening the Auditor General's Office (UNDP-assisted project)
T&T	Telegraph and Telephone
TI	Transparency International
Tk	Taka
UAO	Upazila Accounts Officer
UNCTAD	United Nations Commission on Trade and Development
UNDP	United Nations Development Programme
WASA	Water and Sewerage Authority

Notes

1. At January 6, 2002, Tk 58 = US$1.
2. References to "he", "him", "chairman", etc. are intended to include either gender.
3. Lakh taka = Tk 100,000. Crore taka = Tk 10,000,000.

Executive Summary

This document assesses the quality of financial accountability and transparency in Bangladesh and makes recommendations for improvement. With respect to *public* funds, it compares the financial management standards and practices of agencies using such funds against an international or 'best practice' standard, and also the standards and practices of the external 'oversight' agencies - nine Audit Directorates of the Comptroller and Auditor General's Office (C&AG), parliamentary committees concerned with public expenditure, donor agencies, and the media. It assesses what it would take to qualify the country for programmatic or sector lending in replacement of all individual project lending. With respect to *private* funds in the hands of companies, commercial banks, insurance companies and non-government organizations, it examines the regulatory activities of the Registrar of Joint Stock Companies, the Securities and Exchange Commission, the two Stock Exchanges, Bangladesh Bank, NGO Affairs Bureau and the accounting and auditing profession that serves both public and private sectors.

In recent years, there have been significant improvements in some aspects of fiduciary risk management in the public sector of Bangladesh. Public accounts and audit reports are being sent to Parliament each year and the delay has been substantially reduced. A new budgetary classification system was introduced in 1998: this is making budgets and accounts more useful, particularly for economic analysis. Monthly and annual accounts have been brought much more up to date, and a program is under way to complete the computerization of accounts down to the district level. This will enable public officers to check the integrity of their accounts against the statements of Bangladesh Bank. These are encouraging achievements. Nevertheless, these gains have been offset by a deteriorating control climate.

Currently, fiduciary risk in public spending is assessed as high and would require significant improvement in the public sector financial management before programmatic lending is considered by the donors in the relevant sectors. This is based on answers to standard World Bank and UNDP questionnaires covering: the control environment; planning, budgeting and legitimization of public expenditure; procurement; payroll; disbursements; accounting; external reporting; internal audit; external audit and follow up; and the accounting infrastructure. Interviews, five local consultancy studies and four one-day workshops supplemented the questionnaires. For each major identified risk, recommendations were developed for consideration by the responsible agency. Recommendations were also developed on local government, public enterprises and parliamentary oversight. They are highlighted at the end of each section. Some recommendations have been endorsed at workshops and at an International Conference on Improving Oversight Functions: Challenges in the New Millennium (Dhaka, September 10-12, 2000) organized by the C&AG's Office. Several recommendations are preliminary and directional only, and need more specific development. While it is up to the national authorities to examine the broad spectrum of recommendations, weigh benefits against costs, and develop a financial management improvement program, our analysis suggests that the most serious areas of weakness and the corresponding recommendations are as listed and roughly prioritized below.

Public Sector Control Environment

The internal control climate is poor, as pointed out by the C&AG repeatedly in his reports. Internal controls are the checks and balances in the day-to-day procedures -

procurement, payroll, accounting, reporting and internal audit in each government agency. The Secretary, as Principal Accounting Officer, needs to ensure, with the support of the Chief Accounting Officer and Internal Audit Officer, that procedures are clearly laid down, that officers are trained in them, that records are properly managed and that officers are supervised and corrected where necessary. Where this is low on the scale of executive priorities, frauds and errors multiply like a virus. While there is a lot of emphasis on the improvement of audit, relatively little attention is paid to improving the material audited. A zero-defect philosophy is needed. Initially, a survey of the state of internal control is suggested. This should define baseline levels of internal control and major gaps and lead to a program to strengthen internal controls and visibly enforce the law at all levels. Records management needs to be recognized as a special responsibility in each agency, and officers trained and motivated to upgrade records management practices. Procurement should be separated from receiving, storing and accounting functions.

A public sector ethics code and disclosure of assets rules exist, but are not enforced. Allegations against politicians are rarely if ever independently investigated. Public servants can enrich themselves at public expense with impunity. Pay levels are very low and provide a convenient justification. Public servants and Members of Parliament should adopt a rigid code of conduct, make public statements of assets and liabilities on taking up office, and be given orientation in the framework of public accountability. No one should be above the law.

It is unlikely that the Government on its own would be able to raise levels of accountability and transparency for public funds. A public forum is proposed in which oversight agencies, representatives of civil society and other stakeholders could meet together regularly and review efforts and strategies to build accountability, transparency and the rule of law.

An independent National Accountability and Anti Corruption Commission may be constituted involving members of civil society having high level of integrity. The Members of the commission may be appointed for a fixed term of five years. Once the Government appoint the members of the commission, they can not be removed unless there is any specific case of abuse of power or corruption which must be proved by a three Member Judicial Committee. The Members of the Judicial Committee may be the rank and status of a District Judge. ·

Procurement and Assets Management

The Country Procurement Assessment Report[1] has highlighted the lack of any legal framework, general procurement standards or central authority for public procurement. The result has been widespread misprocurement. Public procurement regulations should be introduced as a first step, and a Department for Public Procurement or Procurement Policy Unit established to take responsibility for procurement standards throughout the public sector. Procurement personnel and evaluation committee members need training and institutional development.

---

[1] World Bank 1999a.

About 30% of public expenditure, and up to 80% of foreign-assisted public expenditure, goes through the procurement process. On paper, contracts for works and services, supplies and consultants are subject to guidelines that follow international standards. In fact, there are many variations in bidding and contract documents, a lack of transparency in the process and long delays in awarding contracts, resulting in higher costs, delayed benefits, nonparticipation of good firms and increased scope for corruption. The Government finds it difficult, acting alone, to enforce its regulations. Donors may assist by setting time limits for award of contracts, after which misprocurement would be declared and funds would lapse. The World Bank has set a standard of eight weeks after the original bid validity period and this has had a positive impact. Transparency would be improved by publishing in the press all awards over a certain threshold value. Creation of an appellate authority is recommended and an Ombudsman to look into complaints of fraud and corruption.

As in other countries that use a cash-based system of accounting, there is a lack of accountability for government assets *other* than cash. Asset registers are not being maintained (except in some donor-assisted projects). This facilitates losses of stores and supplies, and losses and misuse of equipment and vehicles. Proper maintenance of asset registers and periodic independent physical inspections could prevent this.

Internal Audit

Internal audit is nowadays regarded as the first tool of the chief executive officer to ensure effective and efficient operations, reliable reports, compliance with all laws, and the safeguarding of assets. Internal audit should be owned by and report directly to the head of each agency.

In Bangladesh government agencies, internal audit is at an early stage. Units exist only in large ministries and major autonomous bodies and do mainly a pre-audit of transactions. Staff are drawn from line accounting functions, so they are not independent. Performance audits are unknown. There is no central direction or oversight of internal audit standards. The executive management have no technical advice on risk management and control. There is little cooperation between internal and external audit. Both are less effective as a result. The upgrading of internal audit needs to be planned in conjunction with the strengthening of internal control (see above).

Parliamentary Oversight

The development of parliamentary surveillance is one of the main indicators of progress in a nascent democracy. Considerable progress has been made in the brief period since parliamentary democracy was restored in 1991. The principal tools of surveillance with regard to accountability and transparency are the Public Accounts Committee, Public Estimates Committee, Public Undertakings Committee and 35 Standing Committees on individual ministries. These are dominated by members of the party in power. It is difficult for back-bench Members of Parliament to exercise any independent voice as they depend on party favor for appointment to Government office. The constructively critical role of the opposition is not properly understood. Appointments to these Committees, especially the three financial committees, should reflect the need for a broad spectrum of views. In many countries, the chairman of the Public Accounts Committee is an opposition MP with good experience in financial administration. The highest importance is attached to the provision of technical staff and facilities for research and follow-up on Committee recommendations.

The work of the Committees is largely unknown and unnoticed. They are not properly accountable to the House and to the public. Public Accounts Committee meetings should be open to the media and the public, and all committees should submit annual performance reports to the Speaker.

Public Sector Accountants and Auditors

There is a gross imbalance in the distribution of professional Bangladeshi accountants. Only 2% (some 20 chartered and management accountants) work in the public sector and 98% in the private sector. This reflects the very limited role, low status and low pay of government accountants and auditors compared with their counterparts in the private sector.

There are only 20 Chief Accounting Officers for 35 ministries and divisions. Many ministries do not have a full-time chief finance officer. Additional CAOs should be appointed so that each CAO can give undivided attention to his/her agency. Training is not linked with the personnel policies set and administered by the Ministry of Establishment. Personnel are transferred out of the posts for which they have been trained into posts for which they have not been trained. This 'system loss' contributes to poor quality financial management in the public sector. There has not been any evaluation of the impact of training programs of the last few years. Nor has there been any assessment of the needs in the financial management area on which training should be based. It is recommended that the Finance Division and the Ministry of Establishment evaluate past training, survey financial management training needs in the public sector, link training with promotion, placement and transfer policies, and expand the Financial Management Academy program accordingly.

External Audit

The Comptroller and Auditor General is a lynch pin in the system of public accountability to Parliament. He has constitutional independence, and the appropriation for his audit directorates is not subject to parliamentary vote. However, his budget is subject to agreement by the Ministry of Finance and requires adherence to all the administrative circulars and instructions of the Ministry of Finance and the Ministry of Establishment, two of his auditees. His report goes first to the Prime Minister's Office, another auditee. Effectively, he is treated as a part of the executive rather than an independent servant of Parliament. Audited accounts should be submitted directly to the President, with simultaneous copies to Parliament and the Prime Minister's Office.

His audit staff are drawn from the same cadre as the accountants. There is a perception of lack of audit independence. Trained auditors can be transferred back into accounting posts.

To improve the financial accountability in Bangladesh, GoB should take immediate steps to separate the functions of accounting and auditing. The CGA should be given entire responsibility for the accounting function of GoB including controlling all accounting staff. Accounting and audit cadres should also be separated as in other countries of the region. Parliament has no say in the choice of Auditor General. The Public Accounts Committee is the main user of the C&AG's services but is nowhere involved in the nomination process. A C&AG should be appointed as an officer of Parliament for a fixed term of at least five years on the recommendation of the Prime Minister and the Public Accounts Committee.

The above are the most fundamental recommendations in this report. It is based on the new role of the Auditor General in a democracy, that is, as a servant of Parliament rather than of a military regime. Moving his audit functions out of the Executive to a new agency, directly responsible to Parliament, would have a profound impact on the evolution of democracy in Bangladesh.

There is a problem of transparency. Audit reports on Government bodies are not reported to the public (though they are often leaked to the press). The C&AG's annual departmental reports are issued very much later. One way of informing the public of his findings would be to open meetings of the Public Accounts Committee (which receives the C&AG's reports) to the media. His reports would then become public documents.

The C&AG's own accounts are not independently audited. This opens the C&AG to allegations, which reduce public confidence. An independent and expert body should audit the C&AG's accounts.

Major areas of public activity are not audited for lack of staff or expertise. Public audit covers only 16-25% of the C&AG mandate each year. Public revenues are not audited at all. The C&AG has 22,000 auditable units. To complete the audit of this huge portfolio with 3,500 audit staff, most of who are junior staff, is a monumental task. The C&AG and the Government may consider using the private auditors on an experimental basis. Initially, this work may be started with the audit of local Government institutions (City Corporations and Municipalities) and foreign-aided projects. However, the C&AG should be allowed adequate resources to cover the cost of such audits from LGI and project resources. If this is agreed in principle, this should be done by very carefully selected short-listed private audit firms. This approach would facilitate more interaction between private and public sector auditors and accountants and allow them to learn from each other. It would also help to allocate the manpower resources of C&AG to other priority areas of audit and increase the annual coverage of audit.

Public audit standards based on international standards have recently been published but massive training is needed to apply them. The Audit Department needs a strategic plan that addresses these issues of coverage so as to minimize fiduciary risk with the available resources. Training, personnel and transfer policies could then be based on the plan.

Public Enterprises

Public enterprises are responsible for about 40 per cent of all public spending. Their performance has been unsatisfactory at least since 1982. Though their financial performance is considerably dictated by political pricing and output decisions, behind these there is widespread mismanagement, politicized labor relations and corruption. Wages and salaries have been increasing faster than productivity in public enterprises in all sectors. Apart from privatization, which has been dragging slowly, performance can be improved by injecting top-level business experience into the boards. All top appointments should be made on criteria of business experience and track record.

In the last few years, performance 'contracts' between the Ministry of Finance (Monitoring Cell) and some of the larger corporations have been reinforced by a Reward and Punishment Scheme that has added sanctions to the achievement or non-achievement of targets. This has proved that it is possible for delinquent officers to be suspended or even fired. The scheme appears to be having a good effect. It should be gradually extended to all public enterprises continuing under Government ownership.

Nationalized commercial banks still have enormous unrecognized losses on their loan portfolios. Their financial statements and audit gloss over these harsh realities. There is a high risk of illiquidity and need for Government bail-out. Bangladesh Accounting Standard 30 (which is the same as the international standard in all material respects) should be enforced as the accounting standard for bank financial statements. The selection of auditors, their terms of reference and follow-up of audit reports should be tightened.

Cash and Debt Management

Donors have preferred to open special accounts in commercial banks to hold aid funds ready for use in aided projects. These are not within the Government accounting system: accounting is dependent on reports by project directors. Some foreign aid is omitted from the Government consolidated accounts. But these are public funds from the time the donors disburse them. The Bangladesh Bank and C&AG Office need to work out how they can be brought within the public accounts and how balances can be pooled to minimize government borrowing without prejudice to project autonomy and flexibility.

The number of bank accounts holding public funds is unknown. There is a wide distribution of check books on these accounts. A review is needed of the number and distribution of bank accounts and check books with the aim of reducing the risk of illegitimate spending.

There is no law limiting borrowing, nor is there transparent accounting or audit of public debt, contingent liabilities on guarantees, etc. This is a loophole in the system of parliamentary accountability for finance, as ministries can give government guarantees in substitution for present expenditure. All public debt and contingent liabilities should be reported as an annex to the Finance Accounts, and included in the scope of C&AG audit and parliamentary review, in accordance with international standards.

External Reporting

The financial statements of the central government do not meet international standards of disclosure. The public cannot see what has happened to their resources; the cycle of financial accountability is not closed. Financial statements should be prepared according to IFAC standards (or draft standards where final standards have not yet been issued) and published with the audit report.

External reports do not provide information useful in evaluating service costs, efficiency and accomplishments. Few departments report on their performance as required by the Government's Rules of Business. There is a lack of performance accountability – providers of funds cannot assess whether they have been used efficiently or effectively. All public bodies should publish annual reports on performance program-wise.

Reforms in Public Sector Financial Management

There should be political will for major reforms in public sector financial management. To bring significant improvements, steps need to be taken to increase the professional skills of the human infrastructure in the ministries in respect of budgeting, accounting and reporting. In addition, steps are to be taken to increase the use of technology and change the mind-set of the staff through change management training and workshops to use financial management as a tool. (For more details please see the World Bank report 'National Institutional Review', Chapter 2).

The RIBEC family of projects is a success story in Bangladesh in bringing improvements in public sector budgeting, accounting and reporting. These reforms have succeeded through consensus building and participation of the stakeholders. Government may consider building on this success and taking steps for the sustainability of this reform. The financial management capacity in many public organizations, like, Post Office, Telephone and Telegraph Board, Railway Authority and many autonomous bodies is very weak. Steps should be taken to strengthen the financial management capacity of these organizations.

Controlling public expenditures is critical for macro-economic stability and the economic development of Bangladesh. A Public Expenditure Review Commission should be set-up to review the expenditures of the public sector. The Ministry of Finance should work on a short, medium and long-term strategic plan to modernize public sector financial management. The key institutional issues, which are hindering reforms, should also be addressed.

1. Introduction

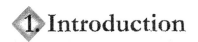

1. Introduction

Context

The People's Republic of Bangladesh is a unitary democratic republic with a written constitution adopted in 1991. The Parliament consists of a single chamber of 330 elected representatives who in turn elect a President, the head of state. The majority party elects a leader who is invited by the President to form the government under his or her prime ministership. The President appoints the Prime Minister and Chief Justice on his own authority. All other executive acts are in accordance with the advice of the Prime Minister, such as appointment of Cabinet ministers. Constitutionally, the Cabinet is collectively responsible to Parliament and the judiciary is independent of the executive branch of government. In fact, the Prime Minister and her party have the balance of power and Parliament and the judiciary are in a constant struggle to assert themselves against the centralized power of the executive.

The constitution requires that all bills for the expenditure of public money be introduced in Parliament by the President. No tax can be levied and no expenditure of public money made except by Act of Parliament. All revenues, proceeds of loans and loan repayments to the Government go into a Consolidated Fund. All other monies received by the Government go into a collection of funds called the Public Account. There is not at present any Act regulating the use of public money. The Constitution says that until there is such an Act, rules made by the President shall apply. The rules put internal financial control under the supervision of the Ministry of Finance. External control is under a constitutionally independent Comptroller and Auditor General (C&AG) who audits all public sector accounts and submits annual and special reports to the President for transmission to the Public Accounts Committee of Parliament. However, the C&AG and his department are administratively subject to the Ministry of Finance and Ministry of Establishment.

As in several other developing countries, corruption pervades all areas of public activity in the country. Administrative inefficiency and reluctance to simplify and streamline procedures are said to be due almost always to underlying corruption. Transparency International and the International Country Risk Guide rate most countries of the world annually and publish corruption perception indices. In 1996, of the 56 countries surveyed, TI ranked Bangladesh as the fourth most corrupt country in the world and ICRG ranked it as the sixth most corrupt country.[1] The report on *Government Malpractices* in the early 1990s confirms extensive corruption in public procurement. Since then, the extent of corruption has by all accounts increased and spread to all levels of bureaucracy and politics. It is the universal view that unless corruption is addressed, other reforms can have only a marginal impact.

Poverty is the biggest challenge facing Bangladesh as it enters the new millennium. There is mounting evidence that poverty is associated with poor governance, where government is less accountable and responsive to citizens. Since the poor lack the resources to give bribes, they do not get equal access to government services.[2] Conversely, improvements in governance are associated with higher per capita income, higher adult literacy, lower infant mortality and reduced poverty.

---

[1] TI and ICRG websites. Bangladesh does not appear in the latest (2000) corruption perception table.

[2] UNDP's 1996 Report on Human Development in Bangladesh: A Pro-Poor Agenda, provides examples of this with reference to education, health services and relief and food aid.

Among donors there is a shift in thinking about the way that aid should be provided. It is no longer considered sufficient to have tightly managed projects, because donor funds are fungible – assistance to these projects permits an increase in government spending elsewhere. The move to a sector and programmatic approach and away from 'ring-fenced' projects has given a new impetus to the call for transparent and accountable governance. Steps towards 'good governance', with a strong emphasis on accountability and transparency, are becoming pre-conditions for aid from the major donors, multilateral and bilateral.

The Government is currently undertaking a number of projects for improvement of accountability in partnership with other donors and NGOs. These include the RIBEC family of projects in the Ministry of Finance, Comptroller and Auditor General's Office and Financial Management Academy supported by UK-DFID; the Strengthening the Office of the Auditor General project and Strengthening of Parliamentary Democracy project, both supported by UNDP; projects of Institutional Support for the Ministry of Finance and the Securities and Exchange Commission, supported by ADB; and a project to strengthen 14 municipalities and two city corporations, supported by the World Bank.

Other initiatives are in the pipeline. The Public Administration Reform Commission has made 137 recommendations,[3] of which the Government has so far committed itself to six. Informal requests for support have been made to the World Bank for: assisting in the implementation of the recommendations of the Public Administration Reform Commission; follow through with the reforms in the National Board of Revenue initiated under the Export Diversification Project (including a Customs Administration Modernization Program); computerization of government payroll and pension systems; the elaboration of an informatics strategy; strengthening the analytical policy work of the Ministry of Finance; and preparation of a standard procedures manual to lay the base for internal controls in central government.

Purpose And Scope

The purpose of the Bangladesh Country Financial Accountability Assessment (CFAA) is to assess the risk that financial resources in Bangladesh may be used illegitimately, inefficiently or ineffectively, by comparing the financial management standards and practices of agencies using (or regulating the use of) funds against an international or 'best practice' standard. This is divided into an assessment of the risk to public funds (public financial accountability) and the risk to private funds (corporate accountability). Assessment of risk requires an assessment of the *internal* controls exercised by the executive on itself, and of the *external* controls exercised by oversight (watchdog) agencies. For both internal and external controls, the risk depends on:

- How much relevant *information* the control agencies can obtain about the use of funds.
- How well they can *analyze* the information and develop action-oriented conclusions.
- What kind of *response* they are able to elicit from the users of funds. Responses are *deterrent* (strengthening of system, punishment of delinquent officers) and *corrective* (recovery of losses, correction of accounts).

---

[3] Public Administration for 21st Century: Report of the Public Administration Reform Commission, 3 volumes, June 2000.

The assessment is a present snapshot. It looks objectively at the risks as they exist now, rather than how far they have changed in the past or how far they are planned to change in the future. It is intended to enable the national authorities to see themselves in relation to best practices and to address their weaknesses through a program of financial management improvement. This report identifies areas of weakness and makes recommendations toward their correction as a first step in a nationally formulated reform program.

The primary emphasis is on legitimacy of use of funds, as defined by legislation and by executive rules, regulations, codes and standards. Efficiency and effectiveness are also concerns, but secondary. In other words, the assessment is more of *financial* accountability than *performance* accountability, though performance aspects are not ignored. No attempt has been made to distinguish the risk of illegitimacy from the risks of inefficiency and ineffectiveness. Most weaknesses contribute to all three.

Structure of The Report

Chapter 2 provides an overview of the 'architecture' of public accountability in Bangladesh – the main players and the accountability cycle. Chapter 3 covers the central government ministries and divisions and their accounts including transactions at district and thana levels. It is sub-divided over the various executive phases and key components of financial management. Chapter 4 deals with the elected local government bodies, which handle public funds – city corporations, municipalities, union councils. Chapter 5 examines public enterprises, comprising the autonomous bodies supervised by the Ministry of Finance Monitoring Cell, the nationalized commercial banks, and the various departmental enterprises such as the Telegraph and Telephone Board and Railway Authority. Chapter 6 examines the main oversight bodies for public funds – the nine audit directorates of the Comptroller and Auditor General's office, the parliamentary committees concerned with financial accountability, donors, and the role of the press. Chapter 7 analyses the accounting and auditing personnel infrastructure in the public sector and their training and discipline. Chapter 8 moves to the private sector, and reviews the accountability of private companies, commercial banks and other financial institutions, and non-government organizations. Chapter 9 covers the private accounting and auditing profession – its structure, standards, training and discipline. Chapter 10 indicates the next steps to be taken. The recommendations are highlighted at the end of each chapter.

2. The Architecture of Public Accountability

2. The Architecture of Public Accountability

Accountability in the Government of Bangladesh is based on a system inherited from former British (1757-1947) and Pakistani (1947-1971) administrations, amended to meet additional needs from time to time, and reaffirmed in the Constitution of 1991 after 16 years of military rule. Articles 81-92 and 127-132 of the Constitution make Parliament the source of all authority to raise revenues and make expenditures and define the role of the President and the Comptroller and Auditor-General (C&AG) and the basic requirements for estimates, demands for grants, charged expenditures, annual Appropriation Acts, supplementary estimates, votes on account and the regulation of public moneys. The functions of the C&AG are further defined in the C&AG (Additional Functions) Act of 1974 and subsequent amendments (Md. Muslim Chowdhury 1999). These include the duty to keep the public accounts and prepare the government financial statements. Thus, the same person is responsible for preparing the accounts and for auditing them – an obvious conflict of interest (see section 7.1 below).

There is no general law or statute setting out the responsibilities for financial management. Detailed rules have been issued – General Financial Rules, Treasury Rules, etc. – as executive orders of the President. These Rules define the responsibilities of the Finance Division of the Ministry of Finance, Secretaries of Ministries and Divisions (who as Principal Accounting Officers are answerable for their respective ministries or divisions[1]), heads of departments, Controller General of Accounts, Chief Accounts Officers, Accounts Officers, Drawing Officers, and public officers generally. Expenditures are subject to pre-audit by Chief Accounts Officers (CAO). If there is any irregularity, the CAO makes the payment but he can raise an objection and inform the Controller General of Accounts (CGA).

The central government financial statements (Finance Accounts) are in two parts - the *Consolidated Fund*, which shows receipts and payments of government money as authorized by the Constitution and each year's Appropriation Act, and the *Public Account*, a group of funds that receive and pay 'other money'. These are published annually together with a supporting statement of actual expenditures compared with budget authorizations, variances and explanations of variances (the Appropriation Accounts).

The budget and accounts for the Consolidated Fund are divided between 'development' and 'revenue'. Broadly, the Development Budget contains all those expenditures that are supported, wholly or partially, by foreign aid/loans. These include capital construction, incremental operating and maintenance expenditures, and technical assistance. The Revenue Budget contains government revenues from taxes, aid and loans, recurrent expenditures insofar as they are not in the Development Budget (typically the staff costs), interest on development loans and some 'non-developmental' capital expenditures such as administrative buildings.

The level of accountability in a country depends on internal controls within the executive branch and external controls exercised by oversight (watchdog) agencies. Internal executive controls in Bangladesh are exercised principally by the Finance Division, which is primarily responsible for maintaining financial discipline throughout the public sector, and Internal Audit Cells, which exist in about a dozen large ministries and in all the sector corporations.

---

[1] Rules of Business (1996) Ch.1, section 4 (vi) says that the Secretary is Principal Accounting Officer, but does not say to whom he is accountable. There is no mention of Parliament.

The oversight agencies are the C&AG (nine Audit Directorates), the parliamentary committees concerned with public expenditure (three financial committees and 35 standing committees on ministries), and the Anti-Corruption Bureau. The Constitution provides for an Ombudsman, and the current government made an election pledge to appoint one, but no one has ever been appointed to this office. The C&AG is the first line oversight agency, examining all public accounts (though in practice he examines only 17-25 percent of all auditable units each year – see section 7.1), while the others are selective investigatory agencies.

The most important is the Public Accounts Committee, which bases its inquiries entirely on the reports of the C&AG. These agencies and their lines of communication are shown in Exhibit 1.

To these may be added the monitoring and evaluation activities of development partners, which apply particularly to the projects they assist and various NGOs in civil society and the media insofar as they concern themselves with public expenditure.

There is little 'horizontal' accountability to beneficiaries of government services, except in some projects in which community-based organizations participate with government agencies in monitoring outputs and outcomes. Almost all accountability lines are up the hierarchical chain through project directors, line directors, department heads, secretaries and ministers to the elected representatives of the people in Parliament. In the elected local government institutions, there is vertical accountability both to elected local councils and vertically to the central government through the Ministry of Local Government.

Public funds are used by central government ministries/divisions, departments of the departmentalized ministries (including Telegraph & Telephone, Postal, Railway, Defense, Forest), local government institutions (city corporations, municipalities and union councils), and public enterprises (sector corporations and their subsidiary enterprises, nationalized commercial banks and development finance institutions).

Bangladesh 'general government' includes about 60 nonprofit institutions controlled and largely funded by the central government, such as the universities. For lack of time, these were not included in the assessment. The Anti-Corruption Bureau is not believed to be effective and was also omitted. Individuals, partnerships, companies (financial and non-financial) and non-government institutions use private funds. Individuals and partnerships were not examined, nor NGOs in any detail. The omissions are not expected to have any significant impact on the report's conclusions and recommendations.

Figure 1

The Architecture of Public Accountability

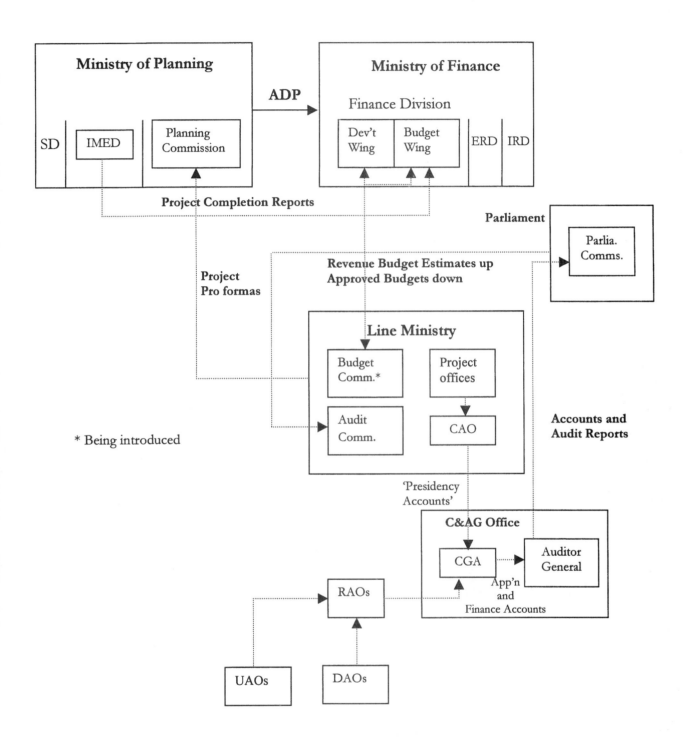

3. Central Government Ministries and Divisions

3. Central Government Ministries and Divisions

The Control Environment

For some time the C&AG has been saying that there is practically no internal control system in the ministries, and that this is one of the main reasons for the staggering number of audit observations. He observes that if structured internal control systems were set up, the audit personnel could do less compliance auditing and more performance auditing.[1]

Internal control is nowadays defined as synonymous with management control, viz. all the methods and measures effected by an entity's management and other personnel to provide reasonable assurance regarding the achievement of objectives in the following categories:

- effectiveness and efficiency of operations.

- reliability of financial and operational reporting.

- compliance with applicable law and regulations.

- safeguarding resources against losses due to waste, abuse, mismanagement, errors, fraud and other irregularities.

General Financial Regulations, Treasury Regulations, Account Code and Audit Code were reissued recently (RIBEC 1996, Ministry of Finance 1998a, 1998b) but not revised or rationalized. All these, together with the Fundamental and Supplementary Rules, the PWD Account Code, the T&T Manual, the Postal Manual, and Forest Manual are outdated and need to be overhauled. Particular procedures need to be rewritten, such as disbursement of pensions.

Accountability starts with every officer being trained in the Regulations, and having ready access to an updated copy. A Rules and Regulations Unit has been set up in the Ministry of Finance, in coordination with a similar unit in the C&AG Office, which will ensure dissemination of regulations. It is then the responsibility of Secretaries, as Principal Accounting Officers, to ensure that officers and personnel are properly supervised and required to comply with regulations.

The Ministry of Finance is responsible for government-wide internal control policies and procedures, and Finance Division is establishing a Financial Information Monitoring Unit, a Coordination Unit, and an Inspection Wing. These are intended to analyze controls, make recommendations on improving controls, act as a change agent in implementation of improvements, and develop in-house capacity to upgrade systems and procedures.[2] Similar units will then be set up in selected ministries. At present, there is no plan for the review and revision of internal controls according to recognized standards such as those of INTOSAI or the Institute of Internal Auditors. The C&AG has proposed a government survey of internal control mechanisms, with a view to expose their deficiencies and devise remedies. This would be a useful first step, which should lead into a program to strengthen controls and visibly enforce them. Records management is poor, as many audit observations relate to absence of records.[3]

[1] Office of the Comptroller & Auditor General Performance Reports 1997:5, 1998:6.
[2] It is not clear why three new units are needed for a single efficiency promotion function.
[3] PAC Third Report, p. 27.

Accountability depends on adequate and accessible records. Good management also depends on orderly records: in fact, files go 'missing' and decisions are made on 'part' files. Records management needs to be recognized as a special responsibility in each agency, and officers trained and motivated to upgrade records management practices.

Transparency implies that records are open and accessible to *citizens*, since government activities are undertaken on their behalf. Currently, records are classified into *Top Secret, Secret, Confidential* and *Restricted*, and the Official Secrets Act makes unauthorized disclosure a criminal offence. The whole culture of government in Bangladesh, as in many other countries, is one of secrecy.[4] A 180-degree cultural shift is required! Freedom-of-information legislation is being introduced in many countries, including India, and is redefining the interface between government and civil society. Instead of defining what can be disclosed, or authorizing release of information on a case-by-case basis, all information becomes publicly available on demand, without question, except for carefully defined exceptions. The technological revolution is facilitating this reform; as a first step, government agencies are putting key documents onto tailor-made websites. 'E-government' is gathering pace. The major constraint is the fear of many civil servants and politicians of loss of discretionary power enjoyed behind the screen of secrecy.

Discretionary power may, of course, be used corruptly. In a recent sample survey of class I and II officers, when they were asked to estimate how much corrupt officials obtained from bribes, the response was a *sevenfold* increase over the official salary.[5]

Rotation of officers is widespread but not regular or systematic. Many frauds are brought to light only when the relevant officers are transferred. A more systematic transfer policy in all posts having access to public funds should be introduced.

Corrective action is conceived almost entirely in terms of recovery of losses from delinquent officers. The strengthening of systems and the punishment of offenders to prevent and deter recurrence of irregularities are a poor second and third. Conflict of interest rules exist but are not enforced. Similarly, the limit on the value of gifts that a public officer may receive is not enforced. Fines can be imposed by administrative action only on junior officers (classes III and IV). Senior public officers and parliamentarians are rarely punished. Cadre rivalry prevents action being taken by a member of one cadre against another. Political protection may hinder effective correction.

The requirements for dismissal of civil servants are very cumbersome. Sometimes the process ends with reinstatement of dismissed officials. They apply equally to employees of public enterprises.[6] Nevertheless, a few public enterprises (Power Development Board, Dhaka Electricity Supply Authority and Petrobangla) have been brought within a Reward and Punishment Scheme sponsored by the Ministry of Finance that has given bonus for achieving pre-agreed targets, and either suspended or removed personnel for culpable failure (see section 5.1 below).

---

[4] The Public Administration Reform Commission (2000) criticised this and proposed a draft Freedom of Information Bill, Vol.1, para. 2.05 and Enclosure 2.1.

[5] World Bank, 2000g.

[6] By a Supreme Court decision, public enterprise employees are also civil servants.

The Prime Minister has required incoming Ministers to make declarations of their assets. These declarations are not made public, but could be used as an internal control. At the Conference on Oversight Functions, it was emphasized that control of public expenditure starts with controls by Parliament on itself. Adequate remuneration, institution of a rigid code of conduct and public statements of assets and liabilities by all MPs on election to office were recommended, together with orientation in the framework of public accountability, particularly on the opening of a new Parliament.

The weaknesses in the control environment are serious deficiencies. Unless public officials' conduct rules and anti-corruption laws are seriously enforced, financial accountability assessment for Bangladesh will remain unfavorable.

Accountability is more effective where the concerned agencies work together. A forum is needed where oversight agencies, together with NGOs and civil society, could regularly review efforts to enhance accountability, transparency and the rule of law, propose new strategies, share information and jointly promote action.

The following recommendations are made:

- **Undertake a survey of internal controls, leading to a program to strengthen and visibly enforce them.**

- **Recognize records management as a special responsibility in each agency, train and motivate officers to improve records management practices, and recognize public right of access to records with defined exceptions.**

- **Institute a rigid code of conduct for public servants and MPs and public statements of assets and liabilities on taking up office, together with orientation in the framework of public accountability.**

- **Establish a public forum of oversight agencies and civil society organizations for the enhancement of accountability, transparency and the rule of law.**

- **An independent National Accountability and Anti Corruption Commission be constituted involving members of civil society having high level of integrity. The Members of the commission be appointed for a fixed term of five years. Once the members of the commission are appointed by the Government, they can not be removed unless there is any specific case of abuse of power or corruption, which must be proved by a three Member Judicial Committee. The Members of the Judicial Committee should be in the rank and status of a District Judge or Additional District Judge.**

Planning And Budgeting

The Government produces Five-Year Plans and an Annual Development Program (ADP). These are the forerunners of an annual Development Budget. The annual Revenue Budget is prepared separately. Annual budgeting is a bottom-up procedure, starting with the preparation of Estimates by government agencies, mainly on an incremental basis from the previous year's approved budget, and culminating in the presentation of the Budget in Parliament by the Finance Minister and its enactment (see RIBEC (1993) and the Country

Profile of Financial Accountability (World Bank 1998b). The budget cycle is summarized in Figure 1.

The budget as a basis for legitimacy

From a fiduciary point of view, the budget establishes the *legitimacy* of expenditures. If disbursements are within the authority provided by the approved budget and in conformity with relevant financial and procurement regulations, donors and citizens are assured that their funds are going into legitimate publicly approved purposes. If public funds can be transferred and spent *outside* the budget, then they are away from public scrutiny. Public funds may flow into private pockets or be used for purposes which stakeholders would not approve. In Bangladesh, there are at least two significant extra-budgetary funds: (1) The Prime Minister's Relief Fund (PMRF), and (2) the Private Fund of the Regiment (PFR). The accountability requirement on each of these funds is that it produces a certificate at the end of the year as to the amount spent.

Managerial efficiency

Budget management is concerned with the value for money achieved with given allocations. A major loss of resource efficiency arises from the organizational and procedural separation of sectoral programs into a 'Revenue Budget' and a 'Development Budget',[7] as there is no formal machinery at the budget scrutiny level to ensure that the operating and maintenance costs of capital projects are estimated and included in the Revenue Budget from the date that they come to completion and are adopted by the Government. The Constitution requires that expenditure 'on revenue account' be distinguished in the overall statement, but this has been misinterpreted as expenditure on projects and activities that are wholly funded by the Government, with no aid component. This contributes to the common syndrome of countries using similar dual budgeting systems: roads without maintenance, hospitals without doctors and schools without books.[8]

Ideally, the problem would be solved by means of a medium-term rolling plan which would bring together, project by project, the respective capital and current expenditures, and match the total expenditure with the projected resources and current fiscal policies. However, a Committee on Reforms in Budgeting and Expenditure Control in 1990 did not recommend the integration of planning and budgeting personnel and procedures, presumably because the major changes in ministry functions and staffing would then have been unacceptable. No changes in ministry responsibilities are envisaged. The RIBEC project is aiming to develop links between the two budget processes through a Medium-Term Budget Framework for the Revenue Budget, and by the use of a common project classification for the ADP and both budgets. It will also be necessary to establish a Joint Budget Committee at the center and Budget Committees at the ministry level, and to develop a networked process that will ensure that all budgets are continuously re-worked on changes in underlying assumptions, such as the timing of project completion. The first steps have been taken in the Ministry of Finance and Ministry of Health where the preparation of estimates is being computerized.

---

[7] These terms are misnomers and should be retired: many recurrent expenditures in the Revenue Budget generate high developmental returns. There is no qualitative difference between allocations for social sectors in Revenue and Development budgets (Kibria 2000). Thus, the revenue/development split has no economic relevance; it is necessary to apply the same economic classification to each budget and consolidate them for economic analyses.

[8] This issue was highlighted in the Public Expenditure Review: 1997 Update (World Bank 1997a: para.10 and Annex IV). Premature recruitment and unnecessarily continued employment of project personnel (ibid. para. 95) complicate it.

Results orientation

A related problem is the poor quality of planning and budgeting. Projects creep into the ADP and budget without due scrutiny: the quality and relevance of projects in the ADP need improvement. Also there is undue reliance on Revised Estimates prepared in the second half of the financial year, which are used to legitimize excess expenditures and reallocate available funds to preferred projects. Budgets are prepared mechanically from previous year data (incrementally) for lack of strategic planning in ministries and divisions, and do not provide any data on the functions, objectives and activities of organizational units, nor their planned progress, outputs and outcomes. Budget scrutiny is similarly incremental. The present procedure does not allow agencies to re-orient their priorities from year to year. Personnel emoluments are usually protected, so cuts apply disproportionately to operations and maintenance expenditures such as travel and utilities, irrespective of their particular impacts on growth, poverty, etc.

This input orientation needs to be complemented by an equal focus on outputs and results. One of the lessons learnt in several countries in the last half century is that such reforms cannot be implemented in a single year (or even five years), nor across the board. Secondly, planning and budgeting is the responsibility of *line managers*, not planning officers and budget officers. The latter are the secretariat only. Thirdly, a result orientation has to start at the top, i.e. with Ministers and Secretaries who are performance conscious and willing to experiment. In a few selected ministries or departments, the Secretaries could start building a medium-term rolling planning process involving all line directors. The RIBEC project has proposed a Budget Committee in each ministry, headed by the Secretary. The Budget Committee could lead and coordinate the planning process. The budget would reflect the first year slice of the plan and would spell out the agreed functions, objectives, outputs, etc. This initiative needs to be actively supported.

A *prerequisite* would be that the Ministry of Finance gives each ministry a budget ceiling (envelope) early enough in the budget cycle that its use could be properly planned, and an assurance that no cuts would be made (except in great emergency). Without this, there is no incentive for a Secretary to undertake detailed planning - that is why they leave it to junior officers. It is believed that earlier estimates of resources are now possible as a result of financial statements being brought up to date. The Resource Committee Technical Secretariat and the new Fiscal Analysis and Monitoring Unit could be made responsible for this. *Donors could play an important role by supporting stable sectoral budget envelopes provided they have assurance that the reform momentum is maintained.*

It will also be necessary to strengthen Management Accounting Units and internal management information systems, subject to resource constraints. RIBEC has sub-projects building up management accounting and MIS support to Secretaries in agricultural services (ASIRP), education (ESTEEM) and health (SHAPLA). Training should be given to senior line managers and their budget and accounts personnel, and Budget Officers in Finance Division, if possible jointly. At a Workshop on Budgeting, Accounting, Reporting and Internal Control on June 24, 2000, participants welcomed a 'corporate' approach to budgeting that would derive budgets from strategic plans and performance indicators in each agency.

Transparency and participation

The planning and budgeting process has been criticized for lack of transparency and lack of consultation.[9] Government agencies have insufficient information to maximize public welfare from their budgets. Parliamentary committees are practically limited to review of public expenditure *after* it has been legislated. The Government's annual budget is normally presented early in June for the fiscal year starting 1 July. This compares poorly with the OECD Fiscal Transparency Guidelines, which say that the budget should be presented to the legislature three months ahead. On the present budget timetable, there is inadequate parliamentary time for scrutiny of the budget before it is passed.

Recommendations in this area are as follows:

- **Make all special public funds transparent and subject to external audit under appropriate arrangements for confidentiality.**

- **The Rules of Business Committee of the Parliament should consider increasing the time allocated to the Parliamentarians for debate on the budget.**

- **Establish 'bridging' machinery to integrate the planning and budgeting process across finance and planning.**

- **Improve the quality of planning/budgeting by decentralizing allocations within sectoral ceilings to ministries/divisions, and instituting strategic planning through Budget Committees.**

- **Donors to support stable sectoral budget envelopes.**

Procurement And Assets Management

Public procurement is estimated at Tk 150 billion a year, of which Tk 100 billion is externally funded, mostly for the public corporations. According to a recent detailed assessment,[10] the perception of practically all observers from the Government, public sector corporations, business community and donor agency personnel is that delays and corruption are endemic and exist at all levels. According to an IMED study covering 148 cases in FY 1998, the average time from inviting bids to awarding a contract was 14 months, resulting in higher costs, delayed benefits, nonparticipation of good firms, and increased scope for corruption. Decisions have to go through an Assistant Secretary, Deputy Secretary, Joint Secretary, Additional Secretary and Secretary and, if they are over Tk 250 million, to a Cabinet Committee for Purchase. Even in public corporations, which are nominally autonomous, contracts over Tk 50-100 million have to get Ministry approval. Donors should set time limits for the award of contracts, after which misprocurement would be declared and funds would lapse.

There is no legal framework for procurement, nor any central agency laying down procurement policy or supervising procurement standards. The Implementation, Monitoring and Evaluation Division of the Ministry of Planning created a Procurement Monitoring Cell in 1994 but this consists of a single officer. The Ministry of Finance issued General Financial Rules in 1998, which outline general principles applicable to the purchase of stores and construction of public works, but leave detailed procedures to the individual agency. ERD has issued a set of

---

[9] See, for instance, World Bank (2000d).
[10] Country Procurement Assessment Report (World Bank 1999a).

Guidelines applicable to all externally funded procurement. Each agency tends to follow these Guidelines in its own procedure manuals for both international and local procurement, but no standard documents are used for goods, works and consultant contracts, nor standard purchase orders for shopping. The Ministry of Roads and Highways is drafting a new contract document for works. A single set of documents should be made standard for all public agencies.

On paper, about 80 percent of procurement is subject to competitive bidding, but in practice implementation is "far from satisfactory". Private sector representatives note that it is virtually impossible to win a contract without paying bribes, and kickbacks between 10 and 15 percent are said to be the norm. Examples abound of contracts being steered to favored individuals and firms by: giving insufficient time for others to prepare their bids; bids received and opened at more than one location; evaluation criteria not stated or, if stated, rarely followed; collusion amongst bidders then award of contract by lottery; physical blocking of delivery of bids by 'outsiders', etc. Recently, some Parliamentary Committees have been probing individual contracts, e.g. the Committee on Estimates has required various Government organizations to supply documentation on all contracts above given thresholds, in some cases scrutinizing invitations, bids and evaluation procedures *before* contracts were given, i.e. a pre-audit. This has uncovered some major irregularities and has probably had some deterrent effect but may constitute interference or obstruction in the operations of government: it risks diluting executive accountability. Lack of transparency in the procurement process results in misprocurement. The Government should publish in the press all awards over a certain threshold.

There is a general lack of procurement knowledge and skills, especially at the working level. Evaluation committee members are not chosen for their technical competence. Where rules are followed, they tend to be followed blindly without regard to getting value for money. Proper records are not kept. A separate training program should be run for personnel having procurement responsibilities and a procurement audit specialization established in the C&AG Department.

There is no independent appeals machinery. Allegations and complaints delay awards. Creation of an appellate authority is recommended and an Ombudsman to look into complaints of fraud and corruption.

Procurement is not segregated from the receiving/storing and accounting functions. There is little skilled stores management. Registers of Dead Stock[11] and the duty on office heads to inspect and certify dead stock twice a year have fallen into disuse. Asset registers are not maintained by most government agencies for vehicles and movable equipment, except in some aided projects. Assets are not periodically physically inspected and compared with registers to verify their safe custody, condition and use. Some departments do not comply with the rule that, on completion of development projects, vehicles have to be returned to the central transport pool. An initial survey is needed to establish what assets are held and where, who owns them and who is accountable for them, and a pilot study undertaken in one or two selected agencies to value the assets and set up a continuing system of control. This will tighten internal control on government property and also facilitate calculation of allocations for operating and maintenance.

[11] Dead stock is inventory other than livestock.

Recommendations therefore cover every aspect of procurement and materials management. They repeat the recommendations of the Country Procurement Assessment Report:

- **Donors to set time limits for award of contracts, after which time the funds lapse.**

- **Pending legislation, prepare and issue Public Procurement Regulations.**

- **Establish a central unit responsible for procurement policy.**

- **Prepare a standard set of bidding and contract documents for all public bodies.**

- **Publish in the press all contract awards over Tk1 million.**

- **Design and implement a procurement and materials management training program for the public and private sector and training for external and internal auditors in procurement audit.**

- **Establish an appeal mechanism.**

- **Give effect to the Ombudsman Law.**

- **Asset survey and pilot study on setting up asset control in selected agencies.**

Accounting

The standards for central government accounting are contained in the Accounts Code (originally four volumes of detailed instructions for accounting and reporting dating from 1938 and supplemented by a mass of circulars), the General Financial Rules, Treasury Rules and subsidiary rules made there under. The RIBEC project has consolidated all these, deleting those that were obsolete, and published a comprehensive new edition (RIBEC 1996, Ministry of Finance 1998a, 1998b). No revision, rationalization or simplification was made, however. The revision of codes and manuals needs to go beyond routine consolidation and should instead result in an overhaul of the inherited procedures and pave the way for modern fiscal systems. This is planned for later. A Rules and Regulations Unit has been set up in the C&AG office, and a counterpart unit in the Finance Division, which will be responsible for the maintenance, development and dissemination of government accounting standards.

Monthly accounts have been brought more or less up to date by the RIBEC project. They are sent to the Finance Division within 6-7 weeks of the month end.

It is claimed that the quality of accounts has also improved, but this is more difficult to measure. All transactions in the Dhaka area (accounted for by 20 CAOs and the Dhaka DAO) are computerized, but transactions at the 64 District Accounts Offices and 400 Thana Accounts Offices on behalf of all the ministries and divisions which operate country-wide are still recorded manually. From these levels they are summarized manually by 20 Regional Accounts Offices (RAOs) and fed into the CGA's Central Data Processing Unit which prepares consolidated accounts. Six RAOs have been upgraded. Not all offices are using the new classification, so CAO offices have to convert their statements before they can be consolidated. The accounts of Defense, Railway Authority, Telegraph and Telephone Board, and Postal Department are also handled manually and fed into the CGA consolidated accounts. Defense accounts have now been converted to the new classification.

A major problem is the omission of considerable foreign-aided expenditure from the consolidated monthly accounts. According to a RIBEC study (1999e), a large proportion of foreign aid fails to be recorded as development expenditure and simultaneously as aid receipts. This is mainly due to (i) expenditure from special accounts (which are outside the government accounting system) not being notified by Project Directors to CAOs and the CGA, and (ii) direct project aid (payments made by donor agencies directly to contractors, consultants, etc) not being brought to account, or only after a long delay. Donor statements do not always distinguish loans from grants, direct project aid from reimbursable project aid, or even the projects for which disbursements have been made. It is expected that the Management Accounting Units being set up in the ministries will ensure more complete reporting of aid expenditures. Donors should support this by providing regular and timely reports of disbursements in accordance with the Government classification.

The accuracy of the government accounts is in doubt. There are major unexplained differences between the bank balance shown in the Government's balance sheet and the balance shown in the scrolls (bank statements) of the Bangladesh Bank. According to a RIBEC study (2000c), the Bank shows *less* than the Government cash book by an amount generally in Tk billions. One would expect the Bank to have a *larger* balance due to checks outstanding,[12] so the unexplained difference is even greater. Even if the difference narrows, it could still include major losses and irregularities, as there may be offsetting errors or fraudulent entries in both sets of accounts – Government and Bangladesh Bank. *Only regular monthly reconciliations can remove this risk.*

The number of transactions is now so high that reconciliation could only be done by a computerized matching of checks drawn and checks encashed, together with appropriate training and motivation. The RIBEC project has established a Central Reconciliation Unit in the CGA's office but progress is necessarily slow as personnel have to be reassured at every step that their interests will not be prejudiced. The program of computerization needs to be extended down at least to the larger district accounts offices. Four DAOs have been computerized so far. The Bangladesh Bank and Sonali Bank accounting systems also need to be computerized. The Bangladesh Bank check payment clearing system and check receipts have been almost completely computerized. The computerization of cash receipts also will assist the process of reconciliation by providing data in electronic form on amounts received directly by the Bank.

The former system of commitment accounting, whereby every purchase order, work order, contract, etc was recorded as a memorandum record at the time of commitment, has fallen into disuse. This weakens expenditure control and cash management, as the volume of commitments in the pipeline is unknown. Control over commitments should be restored.

Expenditures are often misclassified, sometimes to conceal misuse of funds, so financial statements are distorted. The new classification training should be used to ensure that all classifications are correct. Accounts officers need more supervision.

---

[12] Checks are valid for three months, so the float is always large.

Few public servants are paid by check. Most are paid in cash. Payrolls are controlled by collective bargaining agents and there is no physical identification (e.g. by supervisors) of all personnel on the payroll to prevent payment to fictitious persons (ghost workers). Verification of payees is necessary.

There is no payroll bank reconciliation and follow-up of uncashed checks. Ghost workers paid by check are also not discovered. Bank reconciliation by persons not involved in payroll preparation would detect such losses.

Payrolls and pension schedules are prepared mainly manually. Computerization would reduce the opportunities for corrupt gain and yield administrative savings. At the Workshop on Budgeting, Accounting, Reporting and Internal Control, participants recommended that payroll, provident fund and pension systems should be computerized. Billing and accounting systems in the public utilities (WASA, DESA and PDB) should also be computerized: this would reduce the delay in issuing bills and thereby reduce system loss and illicit gains. It was pointed out that there is internal obstruction to computerization.

Another transparency issue arises from the volume of payments that are charged to *suspense accounts* and not cleared promptly to expenditure. These were initially estimated at Tk 15 billion in PWD, Roads and Highways and Public Health Engineering alone (Chowdhury 1998). These payments include legitimate expenditures for stocks not yet used, and expenditures on behalf of other divisions and departments for which the account codes are notified later. Where budgets are used up, however, such expenditures are excess (illegitimate). They remain in suspense unless and until they are charged in a later year against a new budget. In practice these adjustment entries are delayed, even for years. Suspense accounts are also used to hold up and divert funds, especially funds released towards the end of the financial year. In the end-of-year Finance Accounts, therefore, expenditure is under-recorded and the excess is part of the Public Account balances. These balances are not disclosed in Finance Accounts in past years, which showed only receipts and payments. Finance Division should take action to control illegal use of suspense accounts.

Recommendations are as follows:

- **Bring all donor disbursements promptly to account. Donors should provide regular and timely data in accordance with the standard Government classifications.**

- **Reconcile receipts and payments with the bank promptly and explain all differences**

- **Train and supervise accounts officers to classify expenditures correctly.**

- **Re-introduce commitment accounting.**

- **Computerize the payroll, provident fund and pension procedures, and the billing and accounting systems in the public utilities.**

- **Control the use of suspense accounts.**

Cash And Debt Management

The objectives of cash and debt management are: to ensure that sufficient cash is available as and when needed to meet commitments to make payments; to minimize the cost of borrowings, net of the returns on any surplus funds; and to control aggregate cash flows within fiscal, monetary and legal limits.

The responsibility for cash and debt management is divided between Finance Division (Budget Wing), Economic Relations Division (with regard to external flows and debt), and Bangladesh Bank (with respect to domestic flows and debt). The C&AG keeps the accounts, but has no role in cash and debt projections.

Quarterly releases of funds to spending ministries are delayed. Final quarter releases are sometimes received late in June, so they cannot be used (legitimately) within the financial year. These delays indicate poor cash management. Commonly, revenue projections and development allocations are over-estimated and are reduced in the mid-year revisions. Deficits and borrowings are correspondingly under-estimated.

There are no laws limiting borrowing or the government deficit, nor is there any medium-term macroeconomic framework by which the Government undertakes to keep the deficit/GDP ratio within a given limit. Attempts to make better fiscal projections by means of a general equilibrium model have not so far been successful. The Ministry of Finance uses simple rules of thumb for its projections, but appears to be over-ambitious in its growth and revenue forecasts. A Fiscal Analysis and Monitoring Unit is to be set up in the Budget Wing of Finance Division, to report to the Technical Secretariat of the Resource Committee.

The Bangladesh Bank is the Government's bank, and the first lender to the Government. Where it has no branches, the Sonali Bank acts as its agent, receiving and paying government monies on its behalf. The entire cash balance with the Bangladesh Bank is treated as one,[13] though it operates a separate 'window' for each CAO within this balance. Checks do not distinguish Consolidated Fund transactions from Public Account transactions, nor revenue expenditure from development expenditure, nor revenue and expenditure heads. Bangladesh Bank acts solely as a banker, meeting checks that are properly drawn, and has no expenditure control function such as checking aggregate payments against budgets.

There are many bank accounts holding public funds that are not brought within the Government accounts. Most of these accounts have been established at the request of donors to ensure that their disbursements are held safely and are immediately available for the projects they are aiding. Examples are dollar special accounts (DOSA), convertible taka special accounts (CONTASA) and imprest accounts.[14] Some of these are transferred to accounts held by commercial banks on behalf of aided projects. In effect, the Government is lending them public funds interest-free, then borrowing back from them on Treasury bills to cover its short-term

---

[13] There is one General account and separate accounts for Food, Railways and Foreign Aid.
[14] At June 1999, there were 6 CONTASA accounts and 53 imprest accounts (RIBEC 1999e).

deficits. Secondly, accounting becomes dependent on reports by project directors and some foreign aid is omitted from the Government consolidated accounts. The Bangladesh Bank and C&AG Office should work out how these public funds can be brought within the public accounts and how balances can be pooled to minimize government borrowing without prejudice to project autonomy and flexibility.

The paymaster for most central government departments in Bangladesh is the Controller General of Accounts (CGA), who operates the account with the Bangladesh Bank for receipts and payments on both Consolidated Fund and Public Account. The number of branch accounts is not known. Some 5,000 individuals have access to Government check books[15] and it is alleged that checks can be drawn in PWD, Roads and Highways, BTTB, etc. without reference to budget limits.[16] The CGA in association with the Ministry of Finance should review the entire spectrum of government banking arrangements covering a comprehensive census of: (i) bank accounts harboring public money (including project/foreign aid accounts and extra-budgetary bank accounts); (ii) who control and operate these accounts; (iii) what are the sources of receipts into each account and what types of disbursements are made; (iv) the average end-of-the-day cash float in each account; (v) which supervisory authority receives reports on the transactions passing through each account; and, most importantly, (vi) what public interest, if any, justifies continuance of each bank account outside the Treasury. All bank accounts outside treasury control that are not essential should then be closed and checkbooks withdrawn from officials who would no longer need them. The government payment system needs reform to work in harmony with fully consolidated government cash balances in a Treasury Single Account supplemented by a small number of zero-balance or transit accounts for day-to-day payment operations of the CGA's payment offices.

The Economic Relations Division (ERD) of Ministry of Finance is responsible for management and coordination of external debt, and maintains an MIS on all public sector external debt. Private sector external debt is small, but rising.[17] Commitments, disbursements and repayments of external loans and grants are entered in a computerized system (UNCTAD's Debt Management and Financial Analysis System, DMFAS version 5.0). Data originate with ERD except in respect of IMF credits and special borrowings by Ministry of Food, Defense, Biman, Shipping Corporation and Petroleum Corporation These latter are collected from the respective sources and also entered in the database. From DMFAS, data on the projected debt service liabilities are sent to Finance Division for incorporation in the Estimates and the Revised Estimates. Data on donor disbursements and debt repayments and interest are sent monthly to the CGA. Statements from donors are reconciled with the DMFAS data. No reconciliation is attempted with project data.

The Government borrows from the Bangladesh Bank on a standing overdraft arrangement (called Ways and Means Advances). When borrowing goes over the agreed overdraft limit, the Bangladesh Bank issues 91-day Treasury bills on behalf of the Government. These are sold to the commercial banks and to itself. Thirdly, the Bangladesh Bank issues long-

---

[15] RIBEC 1997d, p.16.

[16] All other departments are subject to pre-audit, ie. the checking of each bill by the CAO before payment. The delegation of cheque-writing powers without pre-audit by the C&AG (called departmentalisation) was intended to make Secretaries, as Principal Accounting Officers, more completely responsible and accountable for financial control in their respective ministries and divisions. This has not happened (World Bank 2000b).

[17] See World Bank…There is now a Hard Loan Committee, chaired by the Governor of Bangladesh Bank, which examines all private debt.

term Government bonds with the approval of the Finance Secretary.[18] It is planned to install the ERD system also in Bangladesh Bank for better management of domestic public debt.

There is a lack of transparency in public debt. Loans do not require parliamentary approval in advance. Even *ex post facto* the C&AG does not include debt in his audit report. External public debt is reported annually by ERD to Parliament (ERD 2000).[19] There does not appear to be any reporting of domestic public debt to Parliament. Debt could be reported annually as an annex to the Finance Accounts. This statement should cover both external and domestic public debt, and be classified by type of instrument and sector of debt-holder as required by the IMF in its system of Government Finance Statistics.[20]

There is no reporting of Government guarantees. There is an unknown volume of contingent liabilities hanging over the Government's head, mainly from guarantees to lenders to public enterprises and counter guarantees to the Bangladesh Bank, e.g. Tk 3 billion to Bangladesh Jute Mills Corporation, and Tk 21 billion due to independent power producers from the Power Development Board and Dhaka Electricity Supply Authority (see RIBEC 1993: 134). These potential liabilities should similarly be reported in accordance with international standards of fiscal transparency, such as those of the IMF and OECD.

Recommendations in this area are as follows:

- **Bring special accounts for foreign aid within the Government accounting system.**

- **Review the number and distribution of bank accounts and check books and close inessential accounts and withdraw checkbooks to reduce risk of illegitimate spending.**

- **Include all public debt and contingent liabilities in the Finance Accounts, C&AG audit and parliamentary review.**

Internal Reporting And Monitoring

Management accounting units are being set up in the main spending agencies. In the Ministry of Health and Family Welfare, the Management Accounting Unit (Accounting, Reporting and Information Technology) is pioneering in the development of an internal reporting system, with RIBEC-SHAPLA assistance. Revenue expenditure has yet to be apportioned to projects. The main problem is lack of suitable personnel. This unit has only one officer. Additional staff should be trained and posted to management accounting units.

In the Controller General of Accounts office, budget data are uploaded from the Finance Division database and combined with revenue and expenditure data from the district and thana offices and sent monthly to the respective Chief Accounting Officers. All Secretaries get monthly management reports from their CAOs.

---

[18] There is also internal (or administrative) borrowing by the Consolidated Fund from deposits and other balances held on Public Account. At 30 June 1998, for instance, the Consolidated Fund had borrowed the entire balance of Tk 128 billion held on Public Account (Office of the C&AG 1999, pp.25/6).

[19] At 30 June 1998, external public debt was $14.0 billion. Debt service in FY98 was $578 million (ERD 1999).

[20] We are informed that the Finance Accounts for FY99 include a statement of public debt.

The Finance Division receives monthly reports of expenditure from the Controller General of Accounts. A recently established Financial Information Monitoring Unit analyses these reports. Comparisons with budget are left to the individual ministries and divisions until mid-year, when they are called on to put up their supplementary estimates.

The Implementation Monitoring and Evaluation Division, Ministry of Planning, operates a monitoring system, with formats covering expenditure and physical progress, and undertakes field inspections. 1,000 projects are said to have been inspected by IMED staff in FY00. Results are reported to the National Economic Council. IMED also participates in donor review missions "when asked", but there are problems of travel and subsistence differentials.[21]

Government-wide there are about 1,300 development projects. Project accountants report to their Project Directors, donors, the respective ministry Management Accounting Units, the CAO, the Ministry of Planning, Implementation Monitoring and Evaluation Division, and to the Foreign-Aided Project Audit Directorate. The demands for reports in many different formats are beyond the capacity of Project Directors, many of whom have no accountants or computers. There are problems obtaining data on expenditure by donors. The RIBEC project has designed and field tested a Project Accounting Manual (RIBEC 2000b) that is intended to provide a platform for meeting all these needs. Computers and training assistance will be required for its implementation.

One problem is that there is no sub-classification of projects by *activity*, nor any activity-based costing system by which project expenditures which are common to more than one activity could be apportioned to the respective activities. Most donors expect project financial management systems to be able to report expenditures by log-frame activity, as *this is the level at which output/progress is also measured*. The solution to this problem may come from the further development of Management Accounting Units in the spending ministries.

Recommendation is therefore as follows:

- **Develop ministry capacity to track expenditures to project activities and relate these to results.**

Internal Audit

Internal Audit Cells exist in large ministries such as Works and Education (perhaps a dozen in total), and in major autonomous bodies. The PAC has called for such a unit to be established in each ministry under a Joint Secretary to follow up on its recommendations. Answering C&AG queries and following up on PAC recommendations should be only part of the duties of an Internal Audit Cell. It should also undertake its own independent program of internal audit. Cells are very under-staffed[22] and are often subject to the head of the accounting function. There are no common policies on such issues as operational independence,

---

[21] Director General, IMED.

[22] Ministry of Education Department of Inspection and Audit has been able to audit only 10% of the schools receiving subvention. This is inadequate: C&AG audits found many cases of false reporting and irregularities.

professional competence and training, scope of work, conduct of work, involvement in risk management, reporting or quality review. They have contact with the external audit only on visits from the latter; there is no sharing of work programs or reports, and the C&AG can place little reliance on their findings.

Recommendations are as follows:

- **Extend Internal Audit Units to all ministries/divisions and strengthen existing Internal Audit Units.**
- **Develop central oversight of internal audit standards.**
- **Internal audit units should report to their head of department.**
- **Train internal audit staff in performance audit.**
- **Develop cooperation between internal and external audit.**

External Reporting

On behalf of the C&AG (who is still constitutionally responsible for the form of the accounts), the Controller General of Accounts (CGA) prepares an Annual Receipts and Disbursements Account for the central government as a whole.[23] These are published annually (the Finance Accounts) together with a supporting statement of actual expenditures compared with budget authorizations (the Appropriation Accounts).

The Finance Accounts and Appropriation Accounts are ready in draft within six months of the year end, i.e. the accounts for FY 2000-2001 should be available by the end of December 2001. RIBEC aimed to include the audited accounts for 1998/99 in the budget document for 2000/01. Annual accounts take longer to prepare than monthly accounts as an effort is made after the year ends to complete adjustments, close suspense accounts, and correct mistakes in posting and classification.

The preparation of the accounts for each Ministry/Division is divided between the Chief Accounting Officer (who keeps accounts only for transactions undertaken in Dhaka, called 'Presidency accounts', and who is supervised by the Secretary) and the CGA, who incorporates transactions originating in the districts and thanas, and is supervised by Finance Division, Ministry of Finance. The responsibility for preparing financial statements is divided between the Controller General of Defense Finance (for defense services), the CAO Railways (for railways) and the CGA. The CGA consolidates all these and produces the annual Finance Accounts of the GOB and Appropriation Accounts.

There is no consolidation of central government accounts with local authority accounts to form 'general government' accounts, nor consolidation of general government with public enterprises to form public sector accounts (as is now expected by the IFAC standard on consolidated financial statements). The C&AG (Additional Functions) Act, 1974, requires the C&AG to prepare a general financial statement summarizing the accounts of the Government,

---

[23] Including Postal, Defence and Railways after adjusting their accrual accounts onto a cash basis.

statutory public authorities, public enterprises and local authorities for the last preceding year (article 7). This is not done.

The accounts of both the Consolidated Fund and Public Account are kept on a cash basis. This should be simple but their format is not transparent. Accounting is single entry. The Finance Accounts are receipts and payments accounts, and no GOB balance sheet is prepared and published. The accounts classification introduced by the RIBEC project from July 1998 should enable more meaningful statements to be prepared in future years, to conform to international public sector accounting standards. This has recently been done for the central government budget (RIBEC undated).

The IFAC Public Sector Committee has issued a number of international public sector accounting standards (IPSAS) and draft standards in recent years, covering both cash-based accounting (as in most Government departments) and accrual-based accounting (as in the proforma accounts kept by departments running commercial operations).[24] These IPSAS relate mainly to disclosure through external statements. The C&AG should set up a team of experts to undertake an in-depth review of the form of Government accounts with a view to moving towards compliance with IPSAS standards.

Under cash accounting, the reporting model is a Cash Flow Statement (distinguishing cash flows from operating activities, investing activities and financing activities) and Notes, including a statement of accounting policies, such as the definition of the reporting entity, the point of recognition for receipts and payments, the treatment of reserves and the translation of amounts denominated in foreign currency. Additional note disclosures should include:

- Lists of physical assets and investments

- Borrowings

- Commitments

- Contingencies (guarantees, indemnities and securities)

- Inappropriated payments (i.e. excesses of expenditure over budget)

- Tax expenditures (estimates of revenue foregone because of preferential provisions of the tax code)

- Forecast information.

Bangladesh does not yet report its government finance statistics annually to the IMF in accordance with its GFS system, as about 120 other countries are doing. This requires a reclassification of central government revenue, expenditure and debt, economically and (expenditure only) functionally, in accordance with the GFS standard. This would add to the international comparability of Government data.

---

[24] See IFAC Guideline for Government Financial Reporting (1998), and Financial Reporting under the Cash Basis of Accounting, Exposure Draft 9, issued May 2000, available on IFAC website: www.ifac.org

The Rules of Business of the Government require ministries and other agencies to prepare an annual performance report. Several agencies do not comply (C&AG is an honorable exception). PARC has recommended that every government office required to deliver public goods or services should publish an annual report on the delivery of those goods or services and make it available to the public.[25]

Recommendations are as follows:

- **Review the form of Government accounts and add the disclosures required under the international standard (or draft standard) for government accounting on a cash basis.**

- **All departments to prepare and publish annual performance reports.**

Reforms in Public Sector Budgeting Accounting and Internal Control

There should be political will for major reforms in public sector financial management. To bring about significant improvements, steps need to be taken to increase the professional skills of the human infrastructure in the ministries in respect of budgeting, accounting and reporting. In addition, steps should be taken to increase the use of technology and change the mind-set of staff through change management training and workshops to use financial management as a tool. (For more details please see the national institutional review, World Bank 2000h, Chapter 2).

The RIBEC family of projects is a success story in Bangladesh in bringing improvements in public sector budgeting, accounting and reporting. These reforms have succeeded through consensus building and participation of the stakeholders. The Government may consider building on this success and taking steps for the sustainability of this reform. The Ministry of Finance should work on a medium and long-term strategic plan to modernize public sector financial management. The key institutional issues, which are hindering reforms, should also be addressed. Controlling public expenditures is critical for macro-economic stability and the economic development of Bangladesh. A Public Expenditure Review Commission should be set up to review the expenditures of the public sector.

The financial management capacity in many public organizations, such as the Post Office, Telegraph and Telephone Board, Railway Authority and many autonomous bodies, is very weak. Steps should be taken to strengthen the financial management capacity of these organizations.

---

[25] Public Administration Reform Commission (2000) para.5.39.

4. Local Government

General

This section covers the financial management of local government institutions (LGIs), viz. *city corporations* (Dhaka, Chittagong, Khulna and Rajshahi), *municipalities* (pourashavas, of which there are 198), and *union councils* (union parishads, of which there are 4,472, covering some 85,500 villages). These are all elected bodies. They spend Taka 5-10 billion a year of public funds. The findings in this report are based mainly on a survey that covered a representative sample of city corporations, municipal councils and union councils (World Bank 2000e). Not covered are 64 District Councils (Zila Parishads) and 489 Thana (Upazila) Parishads, which are presently regarded as branches of central government.

Government control, direct and indirect, on LGIs is quite extensive and strong (Local Government Commission 1997, World Bank 1997b), but not effective. A high proportion of LGI revenue comes from central Government. City corporations assess and collect only municipal taxes and other small revenues. The Local Government Commission pointed out in its report that LGIs have not been able to attain financial solvency due to lack of key personnel, inadequate and outdated valuation of holdings for tax purposes, apprehension of losing popularity, widespread tendency to avoid payment of tax, absence of linkage between payment of tax and services provided, narrow base of tax, etc. LGIs at different levels have overlapping revenue jurisdictions, and the Commission recommended that a Finance Commission be set up to rationalize sources of revenue at all levels, and ensure that revenues were commensurate with functions, responsibilities, population, etc.

Training of LGI officers is in the hands of the National Institute of Local Government. This training is said to be practical and effective (though not for training in specialized financial management skills), but under-staffed and under-funded. Recommendations were made in 1997

Box 1
Local Government Financial Management Framework

Municipal councils (in cities and municipalities) and union councils are legislative bodies corresponding to Parliament at the central level. Elected Mayors or Chairmen head them. Each Municipal Council and the Ministry of Local Government nominate and appoint an Executive Committee for day-to-day administration. The Executive Committee is headed by a CEO and is accountable to the Council. Below the Executive Council there are departments, divided functionally. The Union Council organization is very simple, with a Secretary, an Assessor, and a Tax Collector, headed by an elected Chairman.

Each city corporation is governed by its own ordinance, while all municipalities are under the Pourashava Ordinance of 1977 and union councils are under the Local Government (Union Parishads) Ordinance 1983 and Amendments up to 1993. These laws impose a similar framework of accountability on all three levels. Budgets have to be submitted to the Ministry of Local Government, Rural Development and Cooperatives (MLGRDC) (Deputy Secretary for Local Government) for approval. Accounts of receipts and expenditure are to be kept in the prescribed manner and form, and an Annual Statement of Accounts is to be prepared and sent to the Government by 31 December (six months after the end of the financial year). A copy should also be placed "at a conspicuous place in the office [of the LGI] for public inspection". All LGIs are subject to audit by the C&AG. He sends his report to the Government, and a copy to the LGI which "shall forthwith remedy any defects or irregularities and report to the Government the action taken by it".

to expand the training programs of the NILG for both the municipal personnel and the elected leaders (World Bank 1997b: 18,26). The need to expand training in financial management is evident in the low standards of performance and the extent of criticism in audit reports.

Both MLGRDC and LGI officials appear to be in favor of reform of LG financial management, though opposition is likely from Revenue Departments (assessment and collection) and Engineering Public Works Departments as construction contractors are said to be vehemently opposed to all kinds of documentary evidence or other media of accountability (World Bank 2000e). There was a very positive response in favor of progressive computerization.

Local Government Budgeting

As in central government, the budget is divided into a Revenue budget and a Development budget. The budget timetable, procedure and forms are set by the MLGRDC. LGIs are legally required to balance their budgets. There is no Budget Manual.

Revenue budgets go through the Budget/Accounts Section, the CEO, the Council and the MLGRDC. Development budgets start with proposals for projects in each ward. The Chairman/Mayor forwards proposals to Engineering Section for feasibility study and cost estimation. Project estimates are consolidated into the Development budget, which follows the same path of approvals as the Revenue budget. Development budgets appear to observe national priorities such as poverty alleviation and revenue generation. Budgeting of revenue is often highly unrealistic, with actual collections a third of estimates or less. There is considerable potential for improving collection of taxes and rates. Collections in Rajshahi City Corporation in FY97, for instance, were only 44% of current demands issued and only 8% of mounting arrears (Rahman Rahman Huq 1999b). Budgets are always revised during the year. There is no computerization of budgeting, nor any variance analysis procedure. Budgets are treated as a necessary hurdle to getting resources, not a tool of management.

Local Government Accounting

In general, government accounting rules are followed. Some city corporations have accounts manuals. Most corporations and about half the municipalities are doing monthly bank reconciliation. Union councils do not do bank reconciliation. Substantial delays are common in the recording and processing of transactions, which breeds errors and frauds. City corporations and some municipalities are using computers, but mainly for word processing, not accounting. MIS and computerization programs have been recommended (World Bank 2000e).

Only Dhaka City Corporation uses an accrual basis of accounting. This brings revenue arrears, outstanding utility bills and other assets and liabilities into the formal records and subject to the arithmetical discipline of double entry. This increase in control, however, depends on a higher level of accounting sophistication. Dhaka City Corporation is the only LGI that has the services of a qualified accountant. Some others have part-qualified professionals and many have commerce graduates. MLGRDC (Pourashava Support Unit) has recommended an accrual system of accounting for all municipalities, which was prepared as an output of the ADB-supported

Secondary Towns Infrastructural Development projects. However, a recent survey found no evidence of its use (World Bank 2000e).

While it would be better for all city corporations and municipalities to have accrual accounting systems, in the general absence of qualified budgeting and accounting personnel, this could only be a long-term aim. The short-term priority should be to improve the operation of the existing cash-based system and to put it onto a double entry (self-checking) basis. This was recommended by an earlier study (World Bank 1997b) and is repeated here. It is recommended that accrual accounting be piloted in LGIs where there are sufficient trained budget and accounts officers (of at least accounting technician level) to continue its use after the consultants leave. As a first step, introducing commitment accounting so as to permit more effective control over expenditures and the associated cash outflows could enhance the cash-based accounts.

Where the volume of transactions is high, accounts should be computerized in a way that allows accrual modules such as receivables, payables and fixed assets to be added later.

Most LGIs own substantial fixed assets which are not properly maintained, nor recorded in a Fixed Assets Register, nor is their condition and existence periodically checked. Estate Sections of LGIs need training in this.

Local Government Internal Control

In most LGIs (Dhaka City Corporation is again an exception), budgeting and accounting functions are combined in a single department. This opens up the opportunity to cover up misappropriations by budgeting accordingly. Where the number of posts allows, budgeting should be separated from accounts. Sample municipalities had Accounts/ Budget sections ranging from two to six persons.

Projects are implemented by inviting tenders in the prescribed form. The controls are often flouted through negotiated arrangements (World Bank 2000e). Union Councils are not allowed to undertake more than 8 projects a year, and none over Tk 25,000. Engineers monitor work done and give contractors certificates on which they prepare their bills. Bills are checked by Accounts, and recommended for payment by the respective Ward Commissioner, then approved by the Chairman and paid by Accounts.

There is considerable political influence in tax assessment and collection, procurement, and recruitment. Service rules (BSR 1992) are followed. Grade 1 and 2 personnel are recruited by the MLGRDC, while grade 3 and 4 personnel are recruited locally. Organograms are usually available and up to date, though not necessarily appropriate to functions and workloads. Some key positions may remain unfilled for long periods. Job descriptions are rare.

There are no Operations Manuals setting out procedures to be followed and the internal checks that should operate, such as the separation of authorization, recording and custody responsibilities. Together with the absence of job descriptions, this means that responsibility for any action is not formally assigned, thus making it difficult to establish who is accountable. As such, under the present internal control arrangement, there is a risk of misuse of scarce LGI resources. There is a public perception that the misuse of resources in LGIs is more widespread compared to other Government departments.

Local Government Reporting

There is no internal reporting of actual receipts and expenditures against budgets, and no performance monitoring or evaluation. Further computerization, including setting up separate MIS Units, would help to fill this gap.

Dhaka City Corporation prepares an annual Income and Expenditure account and a Balance Sheet. Other LGIs prepare only a Receipt and Payments account. Most annual statements are up to date, e.g. all the sample municipalities had their statements for 1998/99, but the last statements for Chittagong City Corporation were for 1994/95. Financial statements are not published. In a sample of 19 LGIs, only one displayed its financial statements publicly as required by law (World Bank 2000e). None of the LGIs publishes an annual report of its achievements. Thus there is no transparency and accountability of LGI operations to the stakeholders, both local and external. Financial reports should be mandatory and prepared on a predetermined standard basis.

To stimulate institutional and financial reforms, the World Bank, through Municipal Services Project (MSP) is supporting 14 municipalities and two city corporations to undertake, in first phase, a municipal assessment of participating LGIs (a) to identify institutional weakness; (b) to develop a program of operational and financial management improvements, involving administrative and organizational changes which would strengthen the budgeting, financial and accounting system including revenue enhancement measures; (c) to prepare a Financial and Operational Action Plan(FOAP) with agreed institutional and financial performance indicators;(d) thereafter, sign a Municipal Development Agreement with GOB to implement FOAP and agreed physical investment program within an agreed time frame.

Local Government Internal And External Audit

Only Dhaka City Corporation has an internal audit section. It is mainly occupied with the queries and observations raised by the C&AG. Other LGIs have no internal audit, not even on paper. The Ministry of Local Government does not appraise internal controls in the LGIs. Internal audit units should be established in the other city corporations and the larger municipalities, e.g. where annual expenditure is running at more than Tk.10 million. In addition, Audit Committees could be established in city corporations and the larger municipalities, comprising non-executive Ward Commissioners and other designated officials.

The C&AG undertakes external audit of all LGIs and has all the necessary legal powers. Audits are rules-based compliance audits (no performance audits or system-based audits). Audits are conducted by audit teams, which visit and work full time for a period, e.g. 3 weeks for a municipality (grade A) and the year round for Dhaka City Corporation. Audits are confined to LGI offices and do not generally cover development projects in the field. Audit queries that are not resolved on the spot are compiled into a preliminary report, which is sent for comments, then a final report, called 'Broad Sheet report'. The LGI is given 6 weeks to reply. If a satisfactory reply is not forthcoming, the MLG arranges a tripartite meeting (officers from the Ministry, LGI and C&AG) to resolve outstanding issues. Unresolved issues (audit objections) then go into the C&AG's report for transmission to the President and PAC.

The C&AG has 22,000 auditable units to be audited by 3,500 of his staff most of whom are at junior levels. This is no doubt a monumental task to perform effectively. It is believed that with his current level of staffing and skills, it would be difficult for the C&AG to provide quality audit services to LGIs. In many countries, such as the U.K., private sector auditors conduct LGI audits.

Quality is an important issue in private sector audits also. But there are certain private sector audit firms who can provide high quality audit services provided appropriate terms of reference are drawn up and appropriate fees are paid. If it is decided in principle by the C&AG that private sector auditors would be engaged to conduct LGI audits, they should be done by carefully short-listed private firms who are capable of providing quality audit services. All private audit firms for LGI audits may be contracted by the C&AG. The spirit should be to move toward the regulation and quality control of audits and away from audits by the C&AG staff themselves. This approach would help in proper use of already over-stretched C&AG resources and extend C&AG audits in other priority areas.

For these audits, the fees may be paid by the LGIs themselves based on fees approved by C&AG. This arrangement would promote the exchange of knowledge and ideas between private and public sector accountants and auditors. In time, the C&AG may consider contracting out all LGI annual financial audits to the private sector and to make these a basis for performance audits in the LGIs by the C&AG staff.

Audit reports are not published, nor circulated to all Council members. A low-cost recommendation is that MLGRDC should enforce the existing laws and check that annual statements and audit reports are publicly displayed, and take action against delinquent councils. Without this, there is little or no local accountability.

Recommendations are as follows:

- **Publish annual performance reports including financial statements and audit reports of LGIs.**

- **Expand and upgrade training programs in financial management of the National Institute for Local Government.**

- **Improve the cash-based accounting of local government institutions by putting it onto a double-entry system and pilot accrual accounting only in LGIs where there are sufficient trained staffs.**

- Separate budget management from accounting and establish a budget section in each LGI headed by a Budget Officer where there are sufficient personnel.

- Promote progressive computerization of budgeting and accounting, and the introduction of MIS Units to provide data for monitoring and evaluating performance.

- Maintain and update asset registers in LGIs.

- Establish separate internal audit units in city corporations and larger municipalities. In addition, Audit Committees should also be set up in LGIs with adequate representation from civil society and professional groups.

- Harmonization of financial reporting practices in LGIs through mandatory application of standard formats.

- C&AG to contract out some LGI audits to professional firms.

5. Public Enterprises

Nonfinancial Public Enterprises

There are some 200 nonfinancial public enterprises (NFPEs), grouped under 40 public corporations. Together, their spending of public funds is of the order of Tk 200 billion a year (compared with Tk 300 billion by central government). Their value added accounts for 1.8% of GDP, down from 4.5% in 1985. They are involved in all sectors - manufacturing, utilities, transport and communications, trade, agriculture and fisheries, construction and services. At the end of FY99, they had book assets valued at Tk 761.8 billion, financed 32% from equity and 68% from debt. On operating revenue that year of Tk 201.9 billion, value added was Tk 39.1 billion, divided between employee compensation Tk 16.0 billion, depreciation Tk 19.5 billion and operating surplus of Tk 3.6 billion. Their return on total assets, as a measure of economic efficiency in free markets, was only 0.8%. After charging interest and tax, their net financial result was a loss of Tk 4.7 billion.[1]

NFPEs, of course, do not operate in free markets. Their financial performance is largely dictated by policy and operational interventions by the Government, particularly pricing and output decisions. In FY00, their loss was estimated at Tk 31 billion,[2] an enormous increase on the previous year, but of this, Tk 17 billion was due to the Petroleum Corporation keeping its domestic prices unchanged despite higher import costs, and Tk 10 billion was due to the higher output of the Power Development Board (higher output enlarging the operating loss). Behind the administered prices, however, it is recognized that there is widespread mismanagement, politicized labor relations and corruption. Wages and salaries have been increasing faster than productivity in public enterprises in all sectors.[3]

Nonfinancial public enterprises are quasi-fiscal entities, legally separate from the Government, and are not included in the government budget. However they have a number of fiscal effects. They receive equity injections, loans and subsidies from the Government; they repay loans, and pay interest, taxes and dividends.[4] There are also major effects on macroeconomic balances that are off the budget. Supplier credit is guaranteed by the Bangladesh Bank on a counter guarantee by the Ministry of Finance. Where a corporation cannot meet its debt service liability, it borrows further from the commercial banks.[5] Since 1995, all offers of supplier credit have to be cleared by a committee including the Finance Secretary, Planning Secretary and Bangladesh Bank Governor.

NFPEs are governed according to their respective statutes, not by company law. Legally they are autonomous bodies, but the respective ministries appoint their boards of directors and in practice NFPEs are highly regulated by their ministries. All personnel, investment, borrowing,

---

[1] Monitoring Cell, Ministry of Finance, audited actual data.
[2] Kibria (2000).
[3] National Wages and Productivity Commission (1998).
[4] The average annual net flow FY91 to FY00 to NFPEs from GOB has been Tk 7.1 billion. This comprises: equity 8.8, loans (assumed all from GOB) 25.9, subsidies negligible, less loan repayments 12.2, interest 9.5, taxes 2.9 and dividends 3.0. Data from Monitoring Cell are actual flows except for FY99 (revised estimate) and FY00 (budget).
[5] At end FY98, short-term bank loans were Tk 21 billion, and short-term foreign loans Tk 42 billion.

dividend, pricing and major procurement decisions have to be cleared with the ministry. The Ministry of Finance (Monitoring Cell) approves budgets.

Appointments of board members and chief executives are the most important decisions affecting PE performance. The present quality of directors and top executives is very mixed. These personnel should be appointed strictly on their qualifications, experience and track record in business. The procedure in India is for the Minister to make each appointment from a short list of candidates prepared from a central database of qualified personnel. This may be considered for adoption in Bangladesh.

Public Enterprise Planning and Budgeting

NFPEs are subject to a similar planning and budgeting framework to central Government ministries. Each corporation prepares its estimates starting in January, together with its revised estimates for the current year, for which it has the first six months' actual data. About two NFPEs out of three have partially computerized their budget process. All projects have to be approved by the Planning Commission and included in the ADP. Projects that a NFPE is proposing to finance itself are also included in the ADP, but only after the Monitoring Cell has certified to the Planning Commission that the NFPE will have the necessary funds after paying its liabilities (debt service liability, customs duty, etc).[6] The Revenue and Development budgets are submitted through the respective administrative ministries to the Monitoring Cell, which scrutinizes revenue budgets, ensures that they allow for operating and maintenance expenditures arising in projects taken over by the Government, negotiates targets and gives final approval during the March/May period.

About 20 autonomous bodies have been signing annual 'performance contracts' with the Government since the 1980s. These are effectively extracts from the agreed budgets that highlight key operational and financial targets. Informally, they may have added to the operating autonomy of the better-managed corporations, but overall they had no discernible effect on performance. However, in the last four or five years, contracts have been reinforced by a separate Reward and Punishment Scheme that has added sanctions to the achievement or non-achievement of targets (see box). It should be extended to all public enterprises that will continue under government ownership (mainly the public utilities and regulatory bodies) and linked with performance contracts.

> **Box 2**
> **The Reward and Punishment Scheme**
>
> The scheme has so far been applied to PDB, DESA and Petrobangla. For instance, each of the electricity supply units under PDB has a target for system loss. If this is achieved, the personnel working in the successful unit get up to two months' pay as bonus, on a graduated scale. If targets are not achieved, there is a scale of punishments including warning letters, suspension for a period (loss of 50 percent of pay), and removal from the job. A few officers have actually been removed, and 20-30 have been suspended, despite union objections. Many units have received bonus. Head office managers are also in the scheme: their performance is rated on the average performance of their subordinate units. The scheme appears to have been successful.

---

[6] ADP funding may be allowed to important NFPEs even if they cannot meet their debt service liabilities. The project screening does not remove unsound projects, such as the coal-fired power plant at Barakapuria.

Public Enterprise Accounting

All NFPEs keep their accounts on an accrual basis. NFPEs have started computerizing their accounts (about 25 percent done) and payrolls (30-45 percent). Though there are labor fears, slow progress is being made. Bank reconciliation are done manually. There are some failures to complete reconciliations. Auditors report these.

Public Enterprise Procurement

Corporations are graded by size and each grade has limited authority to place contracts. The board of a large corporation, for instance, may sign a contract up to Tk 100 million. Above that limit, proposed contracts have to be approved by its ministry. Above Tk 200 million, contracts go to the Cabinet Committee on Purchase. The great majority of contracts are within corporation authority. Each corporation has its own procurement guidelines, approved by its Board. Corporations follow the PWD Guidelines for works contracts, the guidelines of the Department of Supply and Inspection for local purchases, and the guidelines of the relevant donor for purchases of equipment from aid. Despite the formal appearance of competitive tendering, guidelines are often breached by collusion among bidders, manipulation of tender specifications, etc.

Public Enterprise Internal Control And Internal Audit

There are no procedure manuals. In their place, there is a mass of circulars on various matters such as financial delegation of power, administrative delegation, submission of budgets, investment and the processing of projects. Few corporations have job descriptions. Payrolls tend to be controlled by the collective bargaining agents for labor. One estimate is that payrolls are inflated 10% by ghost workers and days paid but not worked.

Almost all corporations have an internal audit unit. Its role and position in the organization varies: some report to the CEO, some to the Accounts section.

Public Enterprise External Reporting

Most NFPEs submit quarterly MIS reports to their administrative ministries and the Monitoring Cell, comparing their actual revenues and expenditures with the approved budget. A few can only manage half-yearly reports, coinciding with the preparation of revised estimates. Petrobangla and a few others report monthly, with variance analysis. No virement of budget provisions from one item to another is allowed. However, NFPEs cover excesses by delaying paying their suppliers into the following year. Though they keep their books on an accrual basis, this is not always picked up by audit.

All corporations produce annual income and expenditure accounts and balance sheets. Some also produce cash flow statements. They should be subject to the same accounting standards for preparation of corporate financial statements as private enterprises.

Ministry of Finance (Monitoring Cell) produces a consolidated account of the nonfinancial public enterprises each year for the IMF mission in September. This shows an economic classification of the income statement, appropriations and financing, together with assets, equity, debt, employment, and some financial ratios. It covers the last 10 years, including the revised budget for the current year and actual audited data for the previous year.

Public Enterprise External Audit

Apart from internal audit, NFPEs are subject to so-called 'commercial audit', i.e. audit by the C&AG (Commercial Audit Directorate). The statutes of about 30 out of the 40 corporations provide that there should also be audit by two chartered accountants (CA audit). This should be mandatory in all revenue-earning corporations. The C&AG audit is a compliance audit, as for Government ministries. The CA audit is usually the same as for a private firm, i.e. a compliance audit, based on an appraisal of the internal control system, and a financial statements audit. Recently, CAs have been applying international audit standards in these audits.

The NFPE board submits a short list of audit firms to its ministry, from which the ministry selects and appoints the auditors. No firm can audit the same corporation more than three years running. Some ministries have blacklisted particular firms for fraud or negligence, but they have not been banned from auditing other corporations. The Government should exercise its responsibility as a shareholder and ensure reliable audit.

Recommendations are as follows:

- **Appoint directors and chief executives of public enterprises on their business experience and track records.**

- **Extend the reward and punishment scheme to all PEs which will continue in GOB ownership and link it to performance contracts.**

- **Make chartered accountant audit mandatory in all revenue-earning corporations and make it more effective.**

Nationalized Commercial Banks

There are four NCBs. Together they are responsible for about half of the deposits and loans of the banking system. They have their own Acts and fall within the responsibility of the Ministry of Finance. Unfortunately, they are exempt from the main provisions of the Banking Companies Act and hence do not fall under the full jurisdiction of the Bangladesh Bank.

The problems faced by the NCBs stem from poor governance. They are criticized for insider lending, fraud and mismanagement. Moreover, gross interference in management by the

Government and labor unions compound the problems. For instance, the three-year computerization program is moving slowly because of opposition from union leaders.

Recent studies have shown that these banks are not complying with Bangladesh Bank's requirements for provision against loss on their classified loans, nor the capital adequacy requirements (World Bank 1998a). A study made in 1997 showed that about 45% of their loan portfolio was classified as non-performing against which the provision shortfall amounted to Tk.38 billion in FY99. Applying the provision shortfall against the net worth of the NCBs would increase the already negative net worth to a massive negative Tk.71 billion. This is a potential liability of the Government.[7] Only the steady rise in deposits - mainly due to the bumper harvests and substantial remittances from abroad - has prevented a solvency crisis becoming a liquidity crisis. So far, the Government has paid for bank losses by issuing bonds worth about Tk.50 billion. A further Tk.18 billion bonds are to be issued by the Government in FY01.[8] Effectively, these are gifts to loan defaulters.

Bank financial statements give a misleading picture,[9] and audit standards are low. Bank branches may not be audited at all. This is partly due to bad choice of auditors (the Bangladesh Bank list of competent auditors includes 68 firms many of which do not have the special skills or capacity) and partly to inadequate terms of reference of audit. For instance, the TOR should require at least 20 percent of branches to be audited, as in India. Bank audit reports, even where the statement qualifies them that bad loans are under-provided, do not always spell out the effect of this on the reported profit.[10] Yet, no legal case has ever been brought against an auditor by a depositor or shareholder. Nor has the Bangladesh Bank ever disqualified an auditor.

Recently, the ICAB issued IAS 30 as the standard for bank financial statements. This requires disclosure of movements in the provision for bad debts. It has now been issued as a Bangladesh Bank circular and Gazetted. It applies to all banks with effect from their statements for calendar year 2000. The Banking Companies Act needs to be amended for this disclosure standard.

Recommendations are as follows:

• **Bring all banks fully under the supervision of the Bangladesh Bank.**

• **Enforce the international accounting standard on bank accounting.**

---

[7] Indeed, the same applies to the private domestic banks, which would equally have to be rescued, requiring a further Tk.26 billion for 7 private domestic banks alone. In the Budget speech for 2000-01, it was announced that the Government will reduce the percentage of classified loans in the NCBs by taking over the liabilities of the public enterprises (Kibria 2000).

[8] Kibria (2000). Bonds are issued and serviced by the Government, but are assigned to NCBs against specific bad loans and projects. They are included in bank balance sheets as investments and, per contra, as subordinated debt. As such, they are counted as part of the bank's capital and increase the capital adequacy ratio.

[9] Specifically, (a) income accrual is too liberal on non-performing loans, (b) loan classification and disclosure is too lax, provisioning too low, and investments are not valued at their market prices, thus overstating assets and capital, (c) pension liabilities are not calculated actuarially, (d) tax refunds and other receivables from the Government are kept in the balance sheet, even if there is no chance of collection, and (e) inadequate disclosure of lending to directors, staff and their affiliates.

[10] World Bank (2000c).

Departmental Enterprises

These departments – Bangladesh Telegraph and Telephone Board (BTTB), Bangladesh Railway Authority, Bangladesh Post Office and the Ministry of Food, Department of Food and Government Flour Mills – are anomalies. As they are enterprises, earning revenues that are related to their expenditures, they produce commercial accounts on an accrual basis. However, as they have remained as government departments, consolidation of their accounts with the rest of the government requires parallel cash accounts[11] or conversion of their accrual accounts back onto a cash basis. Then, for reports to the IMF, the cash flows of these entities are removed from those of the Government, as they are counted as public enterprises outside general government.

BTTB, for instance, introduced a commercial accounting system that operates alongside the traditional government cash accounting system. The budget for BTTB is not published and budgetary control is largely ineffective. BTTB accounts are 4-5 years in arrears. Accounting responsibilities are divided between the CAO, BTTB and the CAO, T&T. Their respective accounts do not agree. Financial and management reporting is severely hampered. Financial management in these departments needs to be reviewed and computerized.

The budget of the Railway Authority has been part of the Government budget since 1985. It has been making large losses. Since 1998/99 the budget has been prepared under the new classification. Procedures are supposed to comply with the Railway Code and State Railway General Code, but these are out of print as well as out of date.

The Food Account is non-transparent. Neither the budget nor the accounts show operating cost, stock losses and subsidies. RIBEC has made proposals for modernization of budgeting and accounting systems of Food Department, Railway Authority and BTTB (RIBEC 1998b, c and d).

Recommendation is as follows:

- **Restructure the organization and financial management of the departmental enterprises to enable them to render accurate and timely forecasts and accounts on both cash and accrual bases.**

---

[11] Per General Financial Rule 300.

6. Oversight of Use of Public Funds

External Audit

Structural And Constitutional Issues

The Comptroller and Auditor General has a constitutional mandate to audit and report on the public accounts. Article 128 (4) says that the Auditor General shall not be subject to the direction or control of any other person or authority. It is said that generally there is no political interference in what he chooses to audit and that he has free access to records in most cases.[1] Nevertheless, the C&AG is a department within the Ministry of Finance. There appears to be a basic contradiction. Due to his placement, the C&AG is subject to the direction and control of the Ministry of Finance. The C&AG's budget is subject to the same scrutiny as that of ministries and divisions.

In other countries following a similar governance model, Auditors General normally have considerable operational freedom, though not complete financial freedom to create and fill posts.[2] The C&AG's budget (the part of it devoted to audit) is not subject to Parliamentary vote; it is 'charged' expenditure as in other Commonwealth countries. Since the coming of democracy in Bangladesh, the Auditor General's primary duty has been to serve Parliament rather than the executive. However, his office is still part of the executive. Participants at the Oversight Conference pointed out the anomalies that arise from this: his lack of administrative independence, inability to professionalise his office, conflict of interest through the retention of an accounting function, selection of a new Auditor General without input from Parliament, etc. It was recommended that the Auditor General be made an officer of Parliament, that he be appointed on the recommendation of the Prime Minister and PAC, and that his annual budget be approved by the PAC. The UK National Audit Office was recommended as a model for the constitution of his office.

In some other Commonwealth countries, the Auditor General prepares his budget and submits it to the Speaker of Parliament, where it is examined by the Public Accounts Committee, the C&AG's main client. The Auditor General then has sole executive authority over the use of his budget. In Bangladesh, this would be advantageous. It would secure the resources needed by the C&AG, visibly increase his independence, and add to Parliament's 'ownership' of his office. There is no Constitutional bar to this change (Soliman 2000). However, this should be considered only after accounts and audit are separated.

The separation of the audit function implies that the accounts and audit personnel, who form one interchangeable cadre above the level of Superintendent, should be separated into two cadres. How can an auditor be independent and impartial when auditing the work of his cadre colleagues, or even his own earlier work in an accounts post? Every donor is worried by this 'promiscuity' and has pressed for separation. In practice there is some *de facto* separation of the 10,000 accounts personnel, who all come under the Controller General of Accounts, from the 3,000 audit personnel, who fall under the nine directorates of audit. Only the C&AG himself

---

[1] World Bank (2000f). There are a few special funds that are not normally open to the C&AG, such as the extrabudgetary funds mentioned in section 3.2.

[2] There is a strong case for building up the audit directorates because of the high workload. Some 40,000 units spend public funds, comprising 22,718 units within the public sector and some 18,000 NGOs receiving public grants. There are only about 3,000 auditors, and they can cover only about 16% of the total each year. The shortage is most serious at the management level, where there are only 50 cadre officers.

heads both hierarchies. The selection of auditors for audit assignments is said to exclude any officer who had any involvement in the accounts. The responsible Director of Audit prevents any possible conflict of interest. However, this does not reassure those outside the Government: there is no *perception* of independence.

Separation was legislated as long ago as 1983.[3] It was never implemented. The resistance to separation is due partly to the time and trouble of doing it, involving amendments to the Constitution and the C&AG (Additional Functions) Act, but mainly to opposition from accounts personnel who fear loss of opportunities of transfer into coveted audit posts, which have more travel and promotion prospects as well as the power and privileges that come with being an auditor. Nevertheless, it is widely agreed that separation is necessary, and that the only questions are when and how.[4] Separation has been made in almost every other country in South Asia in which accounts and audit were formerly combined (see box). It is recommended that authority be vested in an independent person to study this material, to undertake a local stakeholder analysis,[5] to formulate a plan in negotiation with all the interested parties that would be in the overall national interest, and to supervise its implementation. The output of this appointment should not be another report. It should be total separation of audit from accounts, actual and perceived. It will be necessary for all parties to look for the national interest.

The C&AG is appointed by the President of the Republic on the advice of the Prime Minister without consultation with Parliament. There is no Constitutional bar to the Prime Minister tendering advice after consultation with the Public Accounts Committee and their consideration of the nominee. If (say) a two-thirds majority of the PAC failed to approve the nominee, the Prime Minister could reconsider. This could be written into the Parliamentary Rules of Procedure. The Oversight Conference recommended that the Auditor General be appointed on the recommendation of both the Prime Minister and PAC.

> **Box 3**
> **Separation of Accounting and Audit in South Asia**
>
> In Sri Lanka, there has been separation of accounts and audit for 70 years. The Donoughmore Constitution of 1931 changed the designation of the Colonial Auditor to Auditor General and made that office directly responsible to the legislature. In 1976-80, India also completely split its accounts and audit services at the union level.
>
> Accounts and audit are also separate in Nepal, Bhutan and the Maldives.
>
> In Pakistan, after receiving the inputs of a High Level Committee which examined the financial, legal and administrative implications, the Government has drafted legislation to complete the separation of accounting and auditing and this is expected to be enacted shortly

---

[3] Ordinance XXVIII of 1983, which was an amendment to the C&AG (Additional Functions) Act, 1974, allowed the Government, by administrative direction, to assign the accounting function to ministries and departments (called 'departmentalization').

[4] A Committee looked at this in 1995 and made detailed proposals for separation, which were abandoned. Participants at a Workshop on Public Sector Auditing on June 15, 2000 agreed that a program for separation is in the national interest and should be planned. The Public Administration Reform Commission (2000) has recommended separation, and that the C&AG be left with audit functions only, Vol.1, para.2.12.

[5] Stakeholder analysis is a definition of who would gain, who would lose, and what adjustments could be made so that everyone gains. Where there is a net national gain, a win-win solution is possible.

The C&AG's tenure is protected in the same way as that of a Judge of the Supreme Court. He cannot be dismissed at political will. However, the Constitution requires the C&AG to retire at the age of 60. Since a C&AG is usually appointed only at the age of 57, this leaves a short 3 years for him to realize his vision. More stability in this office is needed. In other countries, the Auditor General is appointed for a fixed term (Thailand 5 years, India 6 years, Canada 10 years). In Bangladesh this would require a Constitutional amendment. The Oversight Conference recommended that the Auditor General be appointed for a fixed term of five to ten years. This would be subject to termination on the same grounds for removal (such as incapacity) as at present.

The Auditor General is constitutionally required to submit his reports to the President (who then causes them to be laid before Parliament, where they are referred to the Standing Committee on Public Accounts). Under the current Rules of Business, the C&AG has been required to submit his report through the Prime Minister's Office. Since this Office is an auditee, this routing is inappropriate. All responsibilities can be met if the Auditor General submits his reports directly to the President, with copies sent simultaneously for information to the Prime Minister and Parliament (Speaker). The public would be informed through PAC meetings if these are opened to the media and the public (see section 6.2 below).

At present, the C&AG accounts are 'audited' by the C&AG's internal audit unit. There is no external independent audit. It is unfortunately true that there are allegations against auditors that they fake subsistence allowance claims, etc. Even if there were no basis for these allegations, it is imperative that the supreme audit institution of the country, which is a pillar of accountability, be subjected to the same independent scrutiny as all other branches of the state. Participants at the Oversight Conference agreed that the Auditor General should be above suspicion, so he needs strong internal controls and an independent audit report on his department. Audit of the audit agency should not be carried out by an auditee, as this would compromise the Auditor General's independence. In Canada and Bhutan, for instance, private accounting firms are appointed to carry out the audit each year. It was recommended that this question be answered in Bangladesh at an early stage. Audit should be conducted by professional external auditors with good experience in government sector audit and having no conflict of interest that might influence their audit of the C&AG Department. The Prime Minister could select them in consultation with the C&AG.

Audit Methodology

Audit methodology has been improved with assistance from a UNDP-supported project (Strengthening the Office of the Auditor General – STAG) and from a DFID-supported project (Reforms in Government Audit – RIGA). The STAG project has brought in audit standards based on those by INTOSAI. These were officially adopted in February 2000.[6] The RIGA project has updated the Audit Code, written manuals for civil, local and revenue audits and given training in these areas.

Since 1997, the C&AG has maintained a 'Grievance Cell' in his office. This is open to any public official to bring his grievance without going through formal channels. Government

---

[6] C&AG (1999).

suppliers can also lodge complaints. Most grievances are on pay and allowances. Some are of a wider nature. In the first three years, 453 complaints were received and 252 were disposed of.

The audit process starts with audit 'observations' (queries or apparent irregularities) in Inspection Reports to the auditees. After correspondence with higher levels up to the responsible minister, serious unresolved issues go into the C&AG's final report. There were 6,761 in FY97, but only 1,109 in FY98 when higher thresholds of materiality were adopted. Issues are categorized as improprieties, loss/damage/wastage by negligence, and willful theft/embezzlement/ fraud/misappropriation. The C&AG Annual Performance Reports highlight some of the most serious and show the total amount recovered and adjusted (missing documentation obtained) as a combined figure, e.g. Tk 8.3 billion in FY98. This was about 1.5 percent of all expenditure, and many times exceeded the cost of audit, about Tk.0.3 billion. The table below shows the widespread incidence of irregularities of all types.

The C&AG is required to see that expenditure has been incurred "with due regard to the

Table 1 Audit Observations on Ministries of Bangladesh in 1997/98			
Ministries	**Impropriety**	**Loss, Damage, Wasteful Expenditure**	**Theft, Embezzlement, Fraud, Misappropriation etc.**
	(Million Taka)		
Agriculture	84	29	1
Civil Aviation & Tourism	28	35	3
Commerce	13	54	7
Communication	16	99	5
Defense	2	32	..
Education	2	69	..
Energy & Mineral Resources	1150	4	5
Environment & Forest	..	8	..
Establishment	3	13	..
Fisheries & Livestock	5	2	..
Finance	24	1438	8
Food	1	57	24
Foreign Affairs	3	..	..
Health & Family Welfare	1201	55	49
Housing & Public Works	102	125	1
Industries	36	16	14
Jute	30	17	2
Land	9	..	..
Local Government, Rural Development & Cooperative	750	22	8
Shipping	54	5	36
Post & Telecommunication	346	188	1
Textiles	3	5	..
Water Resources	320	2	1

Note: The amount mentioned is only representative and does not reflect the overall situation in any particular area
Impropriety: cases of violation of rules and regulations or budgetary stipulations.
Loss, Damage, Wastage: occurrences that are caused by the negligence of duties or inefficiency of management.
Theft, Embezzlement, Fraud, Misappropriation: cases of loss due to willful malpractice by public functionaries.
Source: Annual Report of the Office of the Comptroller & Auditor General, Bangladesh, 1999

avoidance of waste and extravagance". He has been trying to increase the proportion of performance (value-for-money) audit for the last few years. At his instigation, the PAC requested the C&AG to extend performance audits to at least 1 percent of the public sector. The STAG project is completing a performance audit manual and a trainers manual, undertaking pilot performance audits and giving personnel training. About 100 'special audits' have been completed and reported to the PAC. The quality of these audits still falls short, but they are an encouraging development. The cadre officers and staff with the special skills required for a performance approach (particularly in the absence of performance budgeting and accounting) need to be brought together and developed in a dedicated unit rather than scattered throughout the department and be lost by indiscriminate transfers.[7] Recently the C&AG has established a Performance Audit Unit. The experience of Nepal in establishing performance audit may have useful lessons for Bangladesh and should be studied.

Audit Management

Audit planning needs a new approach. At present, there are no permanent teams for specific agencies or types of audit. Audit planning mainly ensures that all auditors get a chance for field visits. Some areas are entirely neglected, e.g. revenue audit. Given the importance to the Government of improving revenue yields, this is a serious gap.

While the choice of units and special subjects to be audited in any year must remain the prerogative of the C&AG, it would be wise to invite the Parliamentary committees, particularly the PAC, to suggest audits in areas in which they are especially interested. This would add to parliamentary interest in the C&AG's reports, and increase the likelihood of debate and follow up.

Additionally, auditors need to join the information revolution and make use of computers in their work, especially their audit planning, reporting and follow up. The STAG project has started a computerized records database.

Training and Professional Development

The main problem with the C&AG audit directorates is not so much the methodology, or lack of independence, but their *lack of staff skills, supervision and quality control*. Even after years of technical assistance and 'capacity building', the quality of audit reports is widely criticized. This is partly a consequence of the integration of the accounts and audit cadre, because auditors are trained and are then transferred to accounts posts. Similarly, officers are trained in (say) performance audit, then posted to teams where they cannot use their training.[8] There is a general lack of integration of training with audit planning. It is probable that much of the training investment in the past has been wasted by not training officers in the job skills required by their posts *and retaining them in those posts*. Training is also subject to all the bureaucratic rules and procedures of the Ministries of Finance and Establishments. The separation of the audit cadre from control by these ministries, as recommended above, would be a first step towards

---

[7] World Bank (2000f).

[8] Out of 90 officers who went through audit training since 1982, only 18 are still working as auditors. Out of 18 who received training in performance audit, only one has been able to use that training (World Bank 2000f).

formulating a strategic plan for the audit department including a coherent training program. At the Workshop on Public Sector Auditing, participants favored development of a strategic plan for the modernization of the C&AG's Department and application of international standards of audit. It is recommended that the C&AG senior management group undertake, together with FIMA and a representative of the Ministry of Establishment, a survey of training needs over the next five years (1) for the accounting function, (2) for the internal audit and other accountability support functions, and (3) the external audit function. This would then be the base for a strategic plan for the department (13,000 personnel).

Training objectives should include gaining a management perspective, so those auditors would be able to assess and report on the *impact* of irregularities on achievement of the goals of the auditee agency. They should be able to apply concepts such as risk and materiality.

There is little understanding at the operational level of the auditing standards recently adopted by the C&AG (1999). FIMA should provide courses in their practical application.

Training needs to be integrated also with other personnel policies such as promotion. At present promotion through the grades depends on seniority and absence of adverse appraisal reports. There is only one promotion bar (written examination). Audit personnel are not generally interested in being trained and have to be paid an inducement. This is possible where aid partners provide funds, but is not sustainable. With autonomy from the Ministry of Establishment, it would be possible in a closed audit cadre to base promotion more on going through prescribed courses and a rotation of practical experience, and not just years of service. Entry-level qualifications should also be re-examined; at present, most audit personnel have no financial background.

Audit Reports

Several reports are made by audit directorates each year, as follows:

Table 2					
Preparation of Reports by Audit Directorates					
		FY97	**FY98**	**FY99**	**FY00**
Annual reports on ministries*		71	191	55	21
Special audit reports		0	0	20	9
Appropriation Account reports		24	2	4	3
Finance Accounts reports		5	1	0	1
TOTAL		100	194	79	34

* These cover 45 ministries and divisions, or parts of ministries/divisions.

The timeliness of audit reports has improved recently,[9] and should improve further now that the C&AG has his own printing unit and is no longer dependent on the Government Printer. With more resources and better planning, the C&AG should be able to reduce the backlog of unaudited projects. Resources should include provision to hire professional firms of accountants, especially in public enterprises, nationalized commercial banks and local government institutions. In some cases, joint public/private teams may conduct audits. This would not only reduce the backlog, but also would infuse valuable skills into the C&AG office and expose commercial auditors to the wider scope of government audit. At a Workshop on Accountancy Profession and Education on June 12, 2000, there was some support for greater use of chartered accountants, and for allowing practical experience in the audit directorates of the C&AG Office to be accepted by ICAB as sufficient to meet their practical experience requirement for admission.

Hitherto, reports have been in a standard short form as follows: "My senior officers have examined the Finance Accounts [or as appropriate] and to the best of my knowledge they are correct". The C&AG is now considering the form of his report to comply with the newly issued Government Auditing Standards (C&AG 1999). A *qualified* opinion should be given if he disagrees or is uncertain about one or more material items in the financial statements, or an *adverse* opinion where he believes that the statements are not fairly stated. If the C&AG is unable to give an opinion on the financial statements due to uncertainty or to a restriction placed on the scope of audit, he gives a *disclaimer of opinion*, i.e. a statement that he cannot give an opinion, together with reasons.

The PAC has said that it does not want audit merely to identify what went wrong but also to suggest remedies. Some remedies are obvious. In other cases, this would require not only competence in the systems approach to audit but also sufficient experience in systems analysis and redesign to be able to make good recommendations. This is a long way from the current reality. It would be better, for the present, that the emphasis be placed on grouping and prioritizing irregularities and audit observations according to their impact on government objectives. It is up to Ministry/Division Secretaries to appraise their weaknesses and take corrective action, including use of the Efficiency Unit being set up in Finance Division where necessary. Secretaries should remain solely accountable as Principal Accounting Officers. Prioritization of audit objections would increase their importance and add to pressure for response from the executive, which is still very disinterested.[10]

The C&AG's reports are restricted until they have been cleared by Parliament (even though their contents are often leaked to the media). They have to be sent to the President, who places them before Parliament, which refers them to the PAC. If PAC meetings were open to the media, as proposed below, this would be an appropriate point for the C&AG reports to be made available generally. They could be published promptly on the Internet, as in a growing number of countries. Alternatively, they could, with parliamentary approval, be published as soon as they are tabled in the House.

[9] All ministry audit reports for FY98 (ie. the year to 30 June 1998) and Appropriation and Finance Accounts reports for FY98 and FY99 were ready for submission to the President in December 2000. The target is to complete reports on all ministries for FY99 and reports for FY00 on nine key ministries by June 2001.
[10] The PAC reported the average delay in taking preliminary steps to meet audit objections, ranging from 19 months in Ministry of Local Government to 148 months in Ministry of Food (PAC Third Report, p.21).

Recommendations are as follows:

- Separate the accounting and auditing functions in a way that would prevent any conflict of interest, actual or perceived . The Government should consider to form a high level committee (not to submit another report) to find out the ways and means and monitor the implementation of this recommendation within a definite timeframe.

- Involve the PAC in the selection process of the Auditor General and amend the Rules of Procedure of the Parliament to this effect.

- Appoint the Auditor General on a fixed tenure of at least 5 years.

- The Comptroller and Auditor General should prepare an Executive Summary of his Report highlighting the major findings. It should me made mandatory for the Government to take corrective actions within a stipulated time. The public should be informed of the major findings and the actions taken by the Government.

- As per Article 132 of the Constitution of Bangladesh, the Comptroller and Auditor General to submit his reports to the President. It should be made mandatory to submit the report to the Parliament, within 60 days from the date of submitting the report to the President.

- Increase the proportion of performance audit through a special unit of trained officers in the C&AG Office.

- Institute independent audit of the audit department.

- Institute revenue audit.

- Prepare a strategic plan for the Audit Department and base personnel training and transfer policies on the strategic plan.

- Conduct training courses on the new Government Auditing Standards.

- Increase interaction with private firms of auditors and the ICAB.

- Set up an Audit Committee in each and every Ministry and government department involving appropriate professional personnel.

- Ensure the financial and operational independence of the Auditor General by

removing his department from administrative and financial control by the Ministries of Finance and Establishment. However, this should be taken as a second-generation reform and should be considered only after accounts and audit is separated.

Parliamentary Oversight

Role of Parliamentary Committees

Parliamentary surveillance of the activities of Government is a pillar of public accountability under the Constitution. It could be said that the development of parliamentary surveillance is one of the main indicators of progress in a nascent democracy. A UNDP-supported project, Strengthening of Parliamentary Democracy, is working with the Parliament on development and modernization of the Parliamentary institution.

This section focuses on the functions, structure, powers and processes of Parliamentary Committees (PCs) with regard to public expenditure control.[11] The principal PCs for this purpose are the Public Accounts Committee (PAC), Public Estimates Committee (PEC), Public Undertakings Committee (PUC) and 35 standing committees on individual ministries (SCMs).

Parliamentary review of the budget before it is passed was discussed in page 27 Review *after* legislation may be before or after expenditure is incurred. As noted in page 29 above, the PEC has been active in investigating procurement transactions before commitments or expenditures were made. Generally, however, review is *ex post facto*. The PAC review is not only after the event, but after the C&AG has reported on it, which may be years later. There is a backlog of 400 audit reports and accounts. This delay reduces the deterrent and corrective influence on the executive as, by the time particular transactions are examined, those responsible have been transferred, or retired or died, and escape having to appear before the PAC. Accountability delayed is accountability eroded.

The division of functions among the Committees is not very clear. The PAC is mainly concerned with the legitimacy of public expenditures, that money is used for the purposes intended and that the regulations were followed. This is also within the mandate of the SCMs. The PEC mandate is to examine the efficiency and economy of expenditures. They need not limit themselves to official policies underlying the expenditures and can make recommendations on alternative policies that would be more efficient. The PUC examines the non-bank public enterprises, but these are also within the ambit of the other financial committees and the respective SCMs. There is no overall coordination in the choice of issues examined and there have been some overlapping inquiries. A Liaison Committee comprising all the Committee chairmen and with the Speaker as Chairman was recommended at the Oversight Conference as a coordinating device. This Committee would also arbitrate on conflicts of jurisdiction.

Composition of Committees

In the present Parliament, the three financial committees and almost all the SCMs are chaired from the ruling party, and membership is usually divided 60% to the ruling party and 40% to opposition parties. (The PAC has 15 members; other Committees have 10). The former practice of having Ministers chair Committees has been discontinued. This still leaves it open to

---

[11] This excludes actions of individual MPs, such as raising questions in the House.

Ministers to sit as members of Committees other than the three financial committees from which they have always been excluded by the Rules. Ministers can still be members of the SCMs and this reduces the freedom of backbenchers to raise matters of public interest. Consideration should also be given to appointing members of the opposition as chairmen of committees.

The most important committee for accountability is the PAC. The PAC could be chaired by an opposition MP so as to ensure the perception of independence from the party in power.

Powers and Resources of Committees

Committees have considerable investigative powers. They can send for persons, papers and records[12] and examine witnesses under oath. They also have as much access to the C&AG as they need; though only the PAC so far has availed itself of his services. The C&AG is Parliament's major informant. Neither the media nor civil society/private sector groups are a source of information for the PAC, unlike in western parliamentary systems, where employers, trade unions, NGOs and professional associations increasingly interact with the parliamentary watchdogs.

Committees vary widely in their level of activity – the current PAC held 94 meetings over a period of 37 months while the Post and Telecoms Committee held only 15. The level of activity, and even more the level of effectiveness, depend largely on the character of the chairman and the research and secretarial support he can beg or borrow. All PCs are grossly handicapped by lack of resources. This can be contrasted with the public funds recovered following investigations; the present (Seventh Parliament) PAC recovered over Tk 2 billion as a result of its first 34 meetings.[13] Following a needs assessment, suitable accommodation should be provided for the Institute of Parliamentary Studies and at least the three financial standing committees. All members should have modern facilities for communication and research, such as individual cubicles equipped with computers having Internet access and standard word processing, email and spreadsheet applications, and adequate research assistance.[14] Chairmen should have secretarial assistance so that proceedings can be recorded and minutes promptly drawn up and circulated. At a Workshop on Parliamentary Control of Public Expenditure (June 4, 2000) and the International Conference on Oversight Functions (September 10-12, 2000) the highest importance was attached to the provision of technical staff and facilities for research and follow up on Committee recommendations. The Public Administration Reform Commission has also emphasized this.[15]

Transparency

There is a serious transparency issue. The Rules of Procedure require that meetings be held in camera. Much of what the PCs do remains unknown and unnoticed by the public and even by other MPs. Except for the PAC, none of the PCs has issued regular reports to the

---

[12] Some Committees impound large numbers of ministry files for long periods of time; others require copies of files.
[13] Third Report of the Standing Committee on Public Accounts (1998), p. 7.
[14] Recently, a Computer User Center has been set up for MPs to have Internet access and individual email accounts.
[15] Public Administration Reform Commission (2000), para. 8.30.

House, such as an annual performance report covering its activities, findings, recommendations and results. Lack of resources is one reason for this. Another reason is that some Chairmen misunderstand their constitutional role and deal only with departmental officers to whom they issue 'directives'. The Workshop on Parliamentary Control emphasized that PCs are not executive agencies and their decisions are only recommendations. If they are ignored, which has frequently been the case, their recourse is through the House, e.g. by asking the Minister in charge to take action. They may ask for Secretaries to report back to them, but if they fail to comply PCs have no enforcement powers. If they were given enforcement powers, it would be a takeover of the executive branch of government. As Committee members gain experience, and as Secretaries are called to explain each year's irregularities, the Committees can follow up on their previous recommendations and ask what progress has been made. However, they need to have a simple system of monitoring and recording actions taken, recoveries and adjustments made, etc. The Oversight Conference recommended that an annual performance report should be required from each PC chairman to the Speaker, and the reports of the financial committees should be debated in the House. In addition, all PAC meetings should be open to the media and public (possibly without television cameras if these would introduce undue political partisanship into the meetings) and the Rules should be amended accordingly.

Parliamentary committee reports do not close the cycle of accountability. The executive should take action on them. In other countries, this is formalized. The executive should be required by law to respond to PAC reports within a fixed period.

Recommendations are as follows:

- **Opposition MP to chair the PAC.**

- **Eliminate the backlog of reports with the PAC.**

- **Clarify the jurisdiction of parliamentary committees with regard to public expenditure control, and set up a Liaison Committee.**

- **Ministerial Committees should ask the concerned ministries to submit the Ministries' Annual Performance Reports along with financial statements including budgets and budgetary control statements.**

- **Undertake needs assessment and improve facilities of parliamentary committees and Members.**

- **Make parliamentary committees more transparent to the House and, particularly the PAC, open to the media and public.**

Oversight by Donor Agencies

Donors are major contributors to public funds.[16] Their fiduciary requirements vary widely. Where donor agencies support defined projects, they have to assure their own stakeholders that their funds are used for legitimate project purposes, and efficiently and

---

[16] Their disbursements in FY00 amounted to $1,575 million. Most of this was aid to identified projects ($1,150 million), with IDA, ADB and Japan as the major donors (ERD data).

effectively.[17] This has to be balanced against the need for recipients to develop their own project management capacity and to take ownership and responsibility for fiduciary outcomes. Most bilateral donors, such as UK-DFID, themselves purchase planned inputs such as consultants, training and equipment, put their own contractors or consultants to manage the projects, and require accounts, reports and audits to comply with their own rules. Most multilateral donors, on the other hand, such as World Bank, Asian Development Bank and UNDP, are moving toward national execution. This puts formal responsibility for management in the hands of the implementing agencies, which manage projects in accordance with their own legal and regulatory frameworks. In practice, governments often prefer to delegate foreign procurement back to the donor, both to save expense and to protect themselves against domestic pressures. Also, national execution is normally accompanied by capacity building efforts that increase fiduciary assurance while leaving responsibility with national project directors.

At present in Bangladesh, almost all aid is project-based and ring-fenced to a greater or lesser extent. Assurance that IDA funds, for example, are used for developmental project purposes is obtained through the receipt of timely project accounts and independent audit reports, including audits of statements of expenditure and special accounts where applicable. Each credit agreement contains standard financial covenants that the implementing agency shall maintain records and prepare annual accounts in accordance with sound accounting practices to reflect the operations, resources and expenditures of the project. The implementing agency is responsible for project management, including appointment of an acceptable auditor. IDA makes disbursements (or reimbursements) only for eligible project expenditures. If acceptable accounts and audit reports are not received within six months of the end of the financial year, disbursements may be suspended.

Earlier accounts would provide earlier warning signals. Interim unaudited accounts should be submitted for the first six months of operation within a further two months. This would provide warning of problems in month 8 instead of month 18+.

In most World Bank projects, the auditor is the C&AG's Foreign Aided Project Audit Directorate (FAPA). Where a project earns revenue or is run by a revenue-earning agency, however, a private audit firm is required for entity audit. Almost all audit reports are received on time. The problem is rather the low quality of C&AG audits (see section 7.1 below), their late start (only after the financial year ends), and their focus on compliance with Government regulations, neglecting World Bank concerns such as the eligibility of expenditures according to loan agreements. There is little or no audit of statements of expenditure. World Bank financial staff have provided training to FAPA auditors. One training target should be that FAPA can undertake a review of internal controls and issue a management letter six months after a project starts.

Auditors should be required to submit copies of their reports by the required dates, or risk disqualification from re-appointment. All audit reports should be reviewed by specialist staff and task/team leaders in donor agencies and comments sent to the implementing agency within one month. The frequency of missions and the level of supervision should be related to the level of fiduciary risk. At present the audit conducted by FAPAD staff is compliance-based. FAPAD

---

[17] Even though this allows the recipient to divert its own resources into uses that may be very unwelcome to the donor.

was provided project assistance of about Taka 30 million by the World Bank and UNDP for capacity development under the Sixth Technical Assistance Project. Under the project, an audit manual was prepared and some staff were trained. Most of the trained staff were transferred and the capacity is almost lost. However, there is considerable development in the quality of audit with regard to formats and presentation of reports. FAPAD is now submitting short-form audit reports and management letters. They also provide separate opinions on Project Financial Statements, SOEs and Special Accounts. However, there is a perception amongst the donors that the quality of most project audits is low, with few exceptions. A discussion is going on amongst the donors to encourage the Government to use private sector auditors in project audits. In some projects, there are provisions to conduct performance/operational audits using private sector auditors. To reduce the pressure on C&AG's scarce resources and increase the coverage of audit of 22,000 auditable units, C&AG and the Government may consider appointing private sector auditors for project audits. Initially, this may start with the audits of projects which are implemented by parastatals, public corporations and enterprises.

The World Bank's Financial Management Initiative (launched in July 1998 under the name LACI) has built up the numbers and professionalism of financial and procurement staff and has added to existing operational policies. Every new project should have specialized staff for financial management and procurement on the task team from preparation to completion. The Financial Management Specialist assesses and reports on the project financial management arrangements at the time of project appraisal and certifies its adequacy (or develops with the implementing agency an action plan to remedy inadequacies), reviews and certifies the adequacy of financial reports, monitors compliance with financial covenants, and initiates necessary actions on audit reports, with guidance and quality control from Regional Financial Management Advisers. The Procurement Specialist has similar responsibilities with regard to project procurement. Quarterly Project Management Reports (PMRs) are required, including expenditure statements and projections, physical progress/output reports and detailed procurement data. If these are certified as satisfactory by financial and procurement specialists and by the team leader, disbursement is made without the need to submit extensive documentation. However, meeting the full PMR requirements has proved difficult: only three projects (out of 11 projects which were approved after July 1, 1998 for which PMR-based disbursement was made effective) have PMR-based disbursement so far. The Bank is currently reviewing PMR requirements with a view to their simplification. More specialist staff (or leveraging their efforts with consultants) and more pro-activity could also increase this proportion.

National policy makers spend considerable time attempting to fulfill donor requirements and coordinate donor actions.[18] It is now generally agreed that establishing duplicate procurement, accounting, reporting and audit systems in a country does not contribute very much to the development of local systems. Their impact on capacity building can even be negative: program implementation units established by donors may suck the more able national personnel out of government service to meet donor accountability needs and weaken government accountability.

The OECD Development Assistance Committee has not, so far, been able to resolve this problem. One response by major donors has been 'partnership' between donors and host governments, such as the UN's Development Assistance Framework and the World Bank's

---

[18] See, e.g. RIBEC 1999c.

Comprehensive Development Framework.[19] A more radical move is toward sector-based 'common pool' aid and away from project 'ring-fenced' aid. This depends on sector donors disbursing their funds in agreed shares into a common pool on the basis of achievements of planned *outputs*, and agreeing on formulae for linking cumulative disbursements to project indicators.[20]

In Bangladesh, the first multidonor sector-wide program is the Health and Population Support Program, which started in 1998. The World Bank leads a consortium of donors, who disburse funds on pre-agreed percentage shares into a pool held by the World Bank. The Government is reimbursed from the pool in accordance with its eligible expenditure on the program, i.e. disbursements are based on inputs, rather than outputs. There is a major problem in procurement, which has recently been recognized as a major constraint impeding program implementation. All procurement under the program is the responsibility of the Ministry of Health and Family Welfare, and has to follow World Bank guidelines. The prior review of tender documents for contracts of $0.3 million or more ($0.1 million in training contracts), and mandatory post review of all contracts involves the World Bank in the process. However, there are long delays. There are also problems of verifying the Government's eligible expenditure. The audit report for FY99 indicates substantial discrepancies between the financial statements reported by the Management Accounting Unit, the Chief Accounting Officer and Line Directors. Donors are also culpable: only four out of 11 donors had provided disbursement information within three months of request.[21] If these problems can be addressed, this approach could be extended into other sectors such as education.

Recommendations are as follows:

- **Early warning of fiduciary problems through interim audits of internal controls and interim unaudited accounts.**

- **Extensive consultations should be made amongst the donors and also with the Government on donor fiduciary requirements to arrive at a consensus towards reducing the transaction cost of aid management.**

- **C&AG, Government and the donors may start a dialogue to use private sector auditors for audits of project accounts. Initially, this may start with the audit of project accounts, where projects are implemented by statutory government organizations. However, the C&AG should be allowed to use project funds to appoint the auditors and act as the regulator and quality controller of project audits.**

- **Donors to support practical training in the Foreign Aided Project Audit Directorate in relation to the agencies implementing the projects they support.**

- **Allocations for supervision to be based more explicitly on risk assessments.**

---

[19] The CDF is intended to put the World Bank's country assistance strategy and other donor country programs into a medium-term framework that is driven by the host country. The philosophy is one of openness and partnership. It is currently being piloted in a few countries.

[20] Ravi Kanbur and Todd Sandler (1999) A Radical Approach to Development Assistance, in *Development Outreach*, Vol. 1, No. 2 (Fall), Washington DC: World Bank Institute. This is being piloted, e.g. in Burkina Faso.

[21] Bangladesh Health and Population Sector Program: Combined Mid-Term Review and Annual Program Review (2000), paras. 4.27/9, 4.36, 4.40 and 6.25.

Role of the Press

In a democracy, a free press is a channel of information on the use of funds and a forum for mobilising public opinion and bringing it to focus on abuses of funds. Like audit, it can have a preventive deterrent effect as well as a transparency-promoting detection effect. Bangladesh have an energetic and outspoken press. There are 300 daily newspapers and 800 weekly publications published in English and Bangla, a few of which have national coverage. Their role as overseers of accountability, public or private, however, has not yet developed far. Levels of professionalism and integrity are low, while dependence on advertising from the government and business sectors is high. Competition for circulation encourages sensationalism at the expense of objectivity. Journalists need professional training in investigative journalism and journalistic ethics and. This would raise their credibility in reporting business and government affairs. This issue is comprehensively discussed in the national institutional review prepared by the World Bank (2000h, page xii and page 25).

Recommendation:

- **Journalists be provided training in investigative journalism and journalistic ethics.**

7. Public Sector Accountants and Auditors

7. Public Sector Accountants and Auditors

Backwardness of Public Accounting and Auditing

Given the size, complexity and public importance of major spending ministries and autonomous bodies, compared with even the largest private sector firms, one might expect Chief Accounting Officers to play a similar role to Finance Directors in the private sector. This is far from the case. Only 2% of the country's qualified accountants work in the Government of Bangladesh (2 ICAB members, 18 ICMAB). This reflects not just the low pay in the public sector,[1] but also the very limited role and low status of government accountants and auditors. Public accounting in Bangladesh, as in other countries, is still in a primitive cash accounting stage of development (Khan 1990). There is little demand for management information and accountants are stuck in their roles as cashiers and bookkeepers. There are only 20 CAOs (for 35 ministries) and their management role lies mainly in keeping their colleagues informed on how much of their budget is still available for spending. CAOs are graded three levels below Ministry Secretaries, a hierarchical status gap that makes communication difficult. In more advanced countries such as Singapore, government accountants are highly trained professionals providing a full range of financial management and advisory services and drawing salaries comparable with the private sector. The issue is one of training and, in time, the professionalization of the accounting/auditing cadre, not just pay parity with the private sector. The initial need is to provide a CAO for each ministry (World Bank 2000b). This recommendation was endorsed by participants at a Workshop on Budgeting, Accounting and Internal Control on June 24, 2000.

There were 12,846 accounting and audit staff in the C&AG's Department as at September 2000, categorized as follows:

Cadre officers enter directly or by promotion from the staff ranks. The Public Service Commission through competitive examination and a foundation (probation) course recruits direct entrants. Accounts officers are recruited without appropriate qualifications such as a commerce degree. They may be graduates in any subject. Allocation of officers to the specialized cadres, such as Audit and Accounts, should

Table 3: Staffing Position of C&AG				
Particulars	Total	Audit Services	Civil Accounts	Military Accounts
Cadre Officers	204	58	73	73
Audit and Accounts Officers	906	338	568	-
Dy. Assistant Finance Controllers	46	-	-	46
Superintendents	1,632	637	779	216
Auditors	1,698	1,698	-	-
Class III officers	6,700	-	5,315	1,385
Class IV officers	1,041	-	873	168
Other support staff	619	619	-	-
Total	12,846	3,350	7,608	1,888

---

[1] Government accountants get typically Tk 15-16,000/month against their private sector counterparts drawing Tk.60-70,000/month. This reflects not only the low pay throughout the civil service after years of compression and erosion, but also inter-cadre rivalries. Accountancy in the public corporation sector has higher status and attracts more accountants (ICAB 39, ICMAB 70, at June 1999).

be based on relevant education, such as degrees in commerce or accounts.

Audit Directorates from among graduates (any discipline) and holders of the Higher Secondary Certificate appoint auditors and Junior Auditors. AAOs and SAS Superintendents are promoted from Auditors and Junior Auditors who pass the SAS examination.

Training

The Financial Management Academy is responsible for all training to the officers and staff of the C&AG's department. It is providing financial management training to other cadres and other departments also. The DFID-supported FIMA project (a sub-project of RIBEC) has proposed a new strategic plan and governance structure.

The project has designed and run various short full-time courses intended to build particular skills such as IT and use of PCs. Trainees who have the potential are sent to UK for further training in government financial management and change management. Links are being established with the Chartered Institute for Public Finance and Accountancy (UK). There are no active links with local training institutions, such as PATC, BIM, ICAB and ICMAB.

The liaison with C&AG is hampered by the lack of a Training Officer with a training plan for that department. It is recommended that a full survey is made of the training needs of the C&AG Department, including determination of names, posts, duty stations, duties, reporting responsibilities, academic level, past training and service history, and that this be used to analyse the knowledge and skills required in each job, and the existing gaps.

Trainees have not yet been followed up and their performance evaluated. It is recommended that an independent survey be made on past trainees to ascertain the impact of training on the indicators used by the FIMA project.

There is no full-time national faculty for these courses. A 3-day course on training has been given to about 180 officers. From these, 40 have been identified and are being used as part-time trainers in FIMA and C&AG (RIGA project).

Training is not linked with the personnel policies set and administered by the Ministry of Establishment. In particular, personnel are transferred out of posts for which they have been trained, and into posts for which they have not been trained. The 'system loss' in training is said to be 80 percent. Secondly, training is not a pre-requisite for promotion, so personnel have no incentive to undergo training and to reach higher standards of performance. On the contrary they have to be given 'perks' of various kinds to be induced to attend courses.[2] Even the top finance positions in the BCS can be reached by seniority, so effort and application are not required and not rewarded. There is a danger that the investment in FIMA is being wasted like so much other (less valuable) training. It is recommended that greater importance be attached to the professionalization of training and the rationalization of training and other personnel policies.

---

[2] Tk 500 a day is paid to trainees, and free lunches are provided. This adds to the demand for the courses.

The pre-RIBEC courses of FIMA continue separately with a faculty of about 14 instructors. They are not trained trainers. They run: a 14 month induction course for PSC recruits assigned to Accounts and Audit (after which they go on a 10 month attachment); SAS Parts I and II examination preparation courses, four months each, focusing on rules and procedures (the pass rate is about 10 percent); a 3-month junior auditors training course and a 4-month senior auditors training course (on which everybody passes); a law course for mid- and senior-level officers; and a course for personnel of DAO and TAO pay offices. These courses are not evaluated. Syllabi and curricula need to be modernized (RIBEC 1997e).

The major constraints on the expansion of training are: insufficient trained trainers; lack of government counterpart capacity (and resource capacity to take trainers and O&M costs onto the revenue budget when the project terminates); lack of space; and readiness of departments to release officers full time (half-day release has not been tried). There is also a geographical limitation, as accounts and audit officers in the districts are not so easily reached. Training officers in Dhaka are reluctant to go out-station. Distance learning possibilities are being examined, but the country's power and telecom infrastructure appears to be inadequate for Internet access to central learning resources.

It would be advantageous if there could be more contacts and interchange with the accounting profession, as planned in the Maldives, such as personnel exchanges between professional firms and the C&AG office (e.g. for special audits and value-for-money investigations), joint seminars, training fellowships for Government officers who have the potential to obtain the CA qualification, adding ICAB and ICMAB to the distribution list for Government circulars relevant to the profession, etc. In the UK, the National Audit Office keeps in close touch with the profession (see box). Under the Bank assistance to ICAB, five accountants from the C&AG Office would be trained in international audit standards, and would then train others.

> **Box 4**
> **Use of Private Sector Accountants by the National Audit Office, UK**
>
> The NAO contracts out 15 percent of its financial audit work to the private sector in order to keep abreast of developments and to manage peaks and troughs in its workload, and to compare costs and standards. It makes use of temporary staff, mostly qualified accountants, to ensure that it is fully resourced at the busiest times. The NAO also contracts out whole value-for-money investigations to consultants.
>
> Source: NAO Report for 1998-1999

Recommendations are as follows:

- **Provide a Chief Accounting Officer for each ministry.**

- **Prepare appropriate financial management procedure manuals and guidelines for use by the Principal Accounting Officers and Chief Accounts Officers.**

- **Conduct a survey of training needs in the C&AG office.**

- Evaluate the impact of past training.

- Link training with placement, transfer and promotion policies.

- Expand training programs for public accountants and auditors.

8. Private Sector Accountability

Companies

The crises in East Asia and elsewhere have pushed corporate governance to the top of the reform agenda in many countries. A corporate governance framework includes *inter alia* the laws and institutional arrangements for making company directors and managers accountable to shareholders while meeting the company's financial and legal obligations to other stakeholders. The main legislation for this in Bangladesh is the Companies Act 1994. Public companies issuing securities are subject also to the Securities and Exchange Ordinance of 1969 and amendments, the Securities and Exchange Act of 1993, and rules issued under these laws.

This framework is intended to protect shareholders and creditors from misuse of their funds by company directors and officers. The Companies Act prescribes minimum accountability and disclosure requirements similar to those in other Commonwealth countries. All limited companies are required to prepare annual accounts, have them audited by chartered accountants, and submit them together with the auditors' report to the Registrar of Joint Stock Companies. Companies listed on the Dhaka or Chittagong Stock Exchanges (presently numbering 221) have to meet the additional requirements of the respective Exchanges and of the Securities and Exchange Commission (SEC). Since 1997, an amendment to SEC Rules has required listed companies to comply with Bangladesh Accounting Standards (based on International Accounting Standards[1]) and their auditors to meet Bangladesh Standards of Auditing (based on International Standards of Auditing).

The position of shareholders and creditors has improved since the share market scams of 1996-1997, but they still lack reliable and timely information. Many companies fail to submit their annual returns to the Registrar or to hold their annual general meetings, and many also fail to pay out dividends despite adequate profits. Minority shareholders get little or no return on their investment. Allegations of insider trading are common. Corporate audit committees, including minority interest representation, do not exist. Priority should be given to the improvement of accountability of the listed companies.

Responsibility for enforcement is shared among the Registrar of Joint Stock Companies, the SEC, the Stock Exchanges, the professional accounting bodies and the judiciary. The involvement of several bodies in corporate accountability complicates enforcement and reduces overall effectiveness. Though there are encouraging signs of these various bodies working together to improve standards of corporate accountability, there are also examples of unilateral action which have not been in the overall interest.

---

[1] IASs and ISAs are adapted for local laws, institutions and terminology. BASs and BSAs meet IASs and ISAs in all material respects. Out of 40 IASs, 24 have been issued as BASs and the remainders are in process of being adopted. Out of 36 ISAs, 22 have been issued as BSAs (World Bank 2000c). The main outstanding IASs are those relating to segment reporting, leases, employee benefits, business combinations, retirement benefits, investments in associates and joint ventures, and contingent liabilities.

Registrar of Joint Stock Companies

The Registrar is the official holder of all statutory reports submitted by companies. Any member of the public may apply to inspect any company's file for a small fee. There are approximately 42,000 companies. Most of these are private companies that are exempted from the obligation to file their financial statements. There are about 2,400 public companies, which are obliged to file their financial statements annually in prescribed formats. The Registrar cooperates with the SEC and has referred some defaulters to the High Court, but decisions can be reversed on appeal to the Government (Ministry of Commerce). More importantly, the Registrar has neither the systems nor the personnel to monitor compliance across the board. The SEC regulates the 221 listed public companies, but the unlisted public companies are an uncontrolled sector. The Registrar has statutory authority to penalize companies for failure to file their annual reports, but penalties are too small (eg. Tk.1 per day of default) and are paid only if a company voluntarily makes a late filing. Even if returns have been made, the files cannot always be readily located. 'Speed' money has to be paid. The Registrar's office urgently needs computerization and strengthening. Corporate penalties should then be increased to effective levels.

Securities and Exchange Commission

The SEC was established only in 1993 to ensure proper issue of securities, protect investors' interests, and control and develop the capital market. It has minimum disclosure standards for initial public offerings. A recent amendment to the SEC Rules requires annual accounts of listed companies to be audited within 120 days of the end of each year and submitted within a further 14 days. A form of audit report has been prescribed by the SEC, but professional accountants object that this does not cover all their legal obligations as auditors and does not comply with the international standard.[2] Half-yearly reports are required within one month of the end of the first half of each year. The SEC can allow delays of up to three months in holding annual general meetings.

The SEC has 3 officers who are professional accountants (including the Chairman) and several part qualified or with master's degrees in commerce, finance or business administration. It has recently been taking action on alleged frauds and against defaulting companies. 12 cases of failure to comply with auditing standards have been referred to the ICAB. (One member's license to audit was suspended). Far more could be done with more trained personnel. The ADB is supporting SEC and stock exchange development.

Dhaka and Chittagong Stock Exchanges

Each Exchange has listing regulations that add to the requirements of the Companies Act, mainly with regard to contents of the directors' report and chairman's report. The exchanges have powers to delist, suspend trading or fine a company.[3] However, they do not have

---

[2] There are significant differences between SEC's Form B and ISA 700, Appendix 2.
[3] If, for a continuous period of three years, its securities are quoted below 50 % of their face value or it has failed to hold an annual general meeting, or if it has not declared a dividend for five years.

the staff capacity to do much more than monitor submission of financial statements and issue reminders and warnings. 90% of listed companies are in fact submitting their half-yearly financial statements on time.[4] The Stock Exchanges also examine brokers' accounts, but do not have the capacity to examine corporate financial statements for compliance with the Companies Act and accounting standards. Effectively, the SEC takes on this responsibility (though it is also resource-constrained). No delistings have occurred since 1997. Under a recent amendment to the SEC Ordinance, the SEC can issue directions to the Exchanges to take action against defaulting companies.

The Institute of Chartered Accountants of Bangladesh

The ICAB Technical and Research Committee is the *de facto* standard setting body in Bangladesh.[5] The ICAB has a legal monopoly of audit services to all companies. Its members are expected to meet a code of ethics and to apply Bangladesh accounting standards (BAS) and auditing standards (BSA) relating to external general-purpose financial statements. These apply to the accounts and audit of all corporate entities registered in Bangladesh.[6] The Companies Act 1994 has not yet been amended to make them mandatory, but for the 221 listed companies, as noted above, both BAS and BSA have been made mandatory by amendment to the 1987 Rules of the Securities and Exchange Commission. The Companies Act should be amended to make

---

Box 5
Corporate Accountability in Sri Lanka

Professional accounting associations in developing countries are adopting and implementing international standards of accounting and auditing (IAS and ISA respectively). In Sri Lanka, the Institute of Chartered Accountants of Sri Lanka (ICASL) has been adopting IAS and ISA since the 1980s. However, as a professional association, it lacked the legal 'teeth' to enforce them, even on its own members. It was also recognized that the newly established capital market regulators should be involved in setting the standards as well as the users of financial statements, such as investors. The initiative was taken by ICASL and the Ministry of Finance to get a law passed, the Sri Lanka Accounting and Auditing Standards Act, No. 15 of 1995. This created an Accounting Standards Committee with wide representation. The Committee reviews new IAS and ISA, drafts Sri Lankan standards (adapting them to local laws, institutions and terminology), and holds public hearings. The final authority for issue of standards is still the ICASL. Standards are then published by the Government. They have become mandatory since 1999 on about 1,000 companies, including banking, insurance, commercial and industrial companies and public enterprises. Small companies are exempted.

Compliance is monitored by a body, the Sri Lanka Accounting and Auditing Standards Monitoring Board, that was set up by the same Act. The Board has 13 members – three nominated by the ICASL, one management accountant, the Company Registrar, the head of the Securities and Exchange Commission, one from the Central Bank, two from the chambers of commerce, one from the legal profession, one banker, the head of the tax authority and one from the universities. Great care is taken to ensure the independence of Board members. Financial statements audited by practising members of the ICASL (as before) have to be sent to the Board. The Board reviews them for compliance. It can receive and act on public complaints and media comments and has wide powers. . It investigates apparent cases of non-compliance with standards and may give directions, impose fines or take legal action in the courts against directors, officers or auditors of the company. Four technical staff are in place. Initially the Board is treading lightly and its role is mainly educational.

---

[4] Estimate by the Secretary, Dhaka Stock Exchange, December 5, 2000.

[5] Members of the Institute of Management Accountants of Bangladesh also prepare company accounts, and the ICMAB would like to participate in the standard setting process.

the standards applicable to all public companies,[7] and the professional institutes need to amend their bylaws to make them mandatory on their members. On professional training and discipline, see chapter 9 below.

It is becoming recognized that setting and monitoring accounting and auditing standards is the concern of users of financial statements and regulatory agencies, as well as the preparers. It is proposed to set up a *National Accounting and Auditing Standards Board* to promulgate, implement and monitor accounting and auditing standards in the future. This would represent regulatory bodies and users of financial statements such as the National Board of Revenue, Registrar of Companies, Securities and Exchange Commission, Bangladesh Bank, Stock Exchanges, legal profession, Chambers of Commerce and C&AG, as well as the ICAB, Institute of Chartered Management Accountants of Bangladesh (ICMAB), the Universities and other stakeholders. It is proposed that ICAB provide secretarial services to the Board. The ICMAB also favors establishment of a Board with these functions. The experience of Sri Lanka should be studied (see box).

Recommendations are as follows:

- **Amend legislation so as to make Bangladesh accounting and auditing standards mandatory on all public companies, and to set up Audit Committees in all listed companies having adequate participation of minority shareholders.**

- **Computerize operations and strengthen the Office of the Registrar of Companies.**

- **Set up a National Accounting and Auditing Standards Board with representation from the users of accounts and regulators as well as preparers, with legal teeth and capacity to enforce standards.**

Commercial Banks and Insurance Companies

Commercial Banks

It has become increasingly clear in recent years that for corporate governance to be effective, banks and their regulators also need good governance. Commercial banks in Bangladesh comprise four nationalized commercial banks (NCBs), 29 private domestic banks (PDBs) and 13 foreign banks. They are regulated by the Banking Companies Act 1991 and circulars issued by Bangladesh Bank from time to time. Section 5.2 above covers the NCBs, and the comments and recommendations there apply to a lesser degree to the private domestic banks.

In 1997, non-performing loans were about 45% of the portfolio of PDBs, the same as for the NCBs, but have since been reduced. The main problems are now with the NCBs and the two private banks (Rupali and Uttara) which were formerly NCBs. The soundness of most banks

---

[6] There are 221 listed companies, some 2,400 unlisted public companies and about 42,000 private companies.
[7] And perhaps private companies and NGOs over a certain size also.

has been severely undermined by insider lending, fraud and negligence. If full provision were made for their bad loans, their capital would be highly negative (World Bank 1998a). This should be disclosed in their accounts for FY2000, the first year of operation of the new bank accounting standard. In July 1999, the Basle Committee on Banking Supervision issued *Sound Practices for Loan Accounting and Disclosure*. This provides guidance to banks and banking supervisors on recognition and measurement of loans, establishment of loan loss allowances, and credit risk disclosures. Bangladesh Bank should endeavor to bring its supervision/regulation system into full compliance with the standards of the Basle Committee on Banking Supervision.

The Banking Companies Act allows banks to make *secured* loans to their directors and their affiliates, and insider lending has plagued the banking sector. In 1999, the Bangladesh Bank restricted the aggregate loans a director could take to half the director's equity investment in the bank. It also prohibited waivers of interest. No new loans could be given, and directors were given a year to adjust their outstanding loans to the new limit, or vacate their posts. 47 have been so vacated.

Insurance Companies

Since the liberalization of this sector, the number of insurance companies has grown from 3 to 62. These are supervised by the Chief Controller of Insurance (CCI), an office under the Ministry of Commerce. The main legislation for insurance companies is the Insurance Act of 1938 and Rules of 1958. Annual audited financial statements have to be submitted on prescribed forms to the CCI within six months of the end of the year, with separate disclosure of data on each type of insurance – life, fire, marine, etc. These audit reports are not considered sufficient as the insurance company appoints the audit firm. Under the Act, the CCI appoints a different firm of chartered accountants to do an annual 'special audit'. The insurance company pays for both audits. If audit reports differ, the CCI may report auditors suspected of fraud or negligence to the Institute of Chartered Accountants. No audit firm has ever been blacklisted. Recently, for the first time, 11 insurance firms were fined (for issuing policies on credit, in breach of the Act).

> **Box 6**
> **The International Association of Insurance Supervisors**
>
> The IAIS consists of insurance supervisors. It is charged with developing internationally endorsed principles and standards on insurance supervision, and with assisting insurance supervisors in implementing those principles and standards through cooperation programs and training. The IAIS recommendations are advisory, rather than binding, on the membership. In September 1997 the IAIS issued the Insurance Supervisory Principles. The IAIS has solicited assistance from the World Bank in distributing the principles, standards and guidance notes to insurance supervisors, and in promoting implementation of the basic standards. Standards are obtainable from the website: www.iaisweb.org

The CCI also licenses insurance agents and may suspend licenses for improper conduct.

The Act and Rules are out of date and do not always meet current accounting and insurance standards (see box). For instance, the Act requires income from interest, dividends and rents to be shown net of tax deducted at source. This is contrary to accounting standards, and results in the understatement of income and expenditure (World Bank 2000c). A draft bill has been prepared by the CCI.

Recommendations are as follows:

- **Make Bangladesh Bank responsible for the supervision of the whole of the banking sector, including the nationalized commercial and development banks.**

- **Bangladesh Bank to enforce the Basle Committee standards and the international accounting standard (now BAS 30) in the financial statements of commercial banks.**

- **Amend the Insurance Act and Rules in line with international accounting and insurance standards.**

Nongovernmental Organizations

The fragile and fragmented development of the formal political institutions of Bangladesh, coupled with trends in donor aid, have driven the emergence and growth of numerous NGOs. They fall into two main categories – microcredit activities, which are mainly self-financing, and grant-financed delivery of social services and advocacy. There are 1,544 NGOs in receipt of foreign funds registered with the NGO Affairs Bureau (Prime Minister's Office), of which about 1,000 undertake microcredit activities. These NGOs are running 795 projects. In addition, there are about 22,000 locally funded voluntary organizations registered with the Social Services Department.[8] There are several umbrella organizations, of which the most important is the Association of Development Agencies in Bangladesh (ADAB).

NGOs receiving foreign funding are subject to the tight accountability requirements of the respective donors. The larger NGOs readily make available their audited accounts and reports and are said to have fairly good accountability and transparency toward their donors, though there is scope for improvement.[9] ADAB should identify and promote good governance practices.

NGOs are also subject to government control but this is "cursory at best".[10] Those in receipt of foreign funds are subject to the Foreign Donations (Voluntary Activities) Regulation Ordinance, 1978, and Rules under the Ordinance, administered by the NGO Affairs Bureau. The voluntary organizations are subject to the Societies Act of 1961 and Rules made under that Act. The Government's regulatory framework is mainly concerned with ensuring that NGO activities are lawful, do not conflict with government policies and do not duplicate programs in the same villages and functional areas, and to do this without delaying implementation. Funds from

---

[8] Data from the NGO Affairs Bureau, as at December 11, 2000.
[9] DfID (2000) Partners in Development: A Review of Big NGOs in Bangladesh, April
[10] DfID Report, p.42.

donors are sent directly to NGOs' bank accounts, but they cannot lawfully be drawn on until the Bureau has approved the relevant project. NGOs are required to submit their project proposals to the Bureau, which consults with the relevant government ministries and gives clearance to NGOs' banks holding donor funds to allow withdrawals. The Bureau is subject to time limits — applications for project approval have to be answered within 21 days (relief projects within 24 hours).[11] If a bank pays out without Bureau approval, it is disciplined through the Bangladesh Bank. Recently, ADB has made a study on modalities of donor funding and this is under discussion by the Government.

The Rules lay down the books to be kept. Annual accounts are required and audit is by chartered accountants selected by the NGO from an approved list of 150. Audit reports are due within two months of the end of each financial year. The Ordinance empowers the Government to inspect NGO books and to carry out its own audits if necessary. *Annual reports* must also be submitted to the Bureau, showing *inter alia* project outputs and expenditure thana- and district-wise, foreign travel, and emoluments of all employees receiving more than Tk 5,000/month.

Most financial statements, audit reports and annual reports are said to be rendered on time, though the larger and more powerful NGOs tend to act independently. 89% of donor funding goes to just four very large NGOs.

There is a problem of inter-NGO coordination: the proliferation of microcredit NGOs may result in eight or ten working in the same village. Competition is not necessarily beneficial. Borrowers can repay one NGO by borrowing from another. A recent Committee recommended that the Bangladesh Bank and a national NGO monitoring authority supervise NGOs dealing with microcredit. As with government service delivery, the public right to information is the key.[12]

The rules require only double entry accounting and NGO practices are very varied. Some use cash accounting, some accrual accounting. Donors usually demand project-based accounting that shows separately the use of their funds. Donations in kind such as equipment may be treated as income in the year of receipt or prorated over the years of benefit. Some NGOs observe the international standard on accounting for government grants, but most do not. Microcredit institutions should move toward bank accounting practice.[13] It would be better for all NGOs to observe international accounting standards. It is therefore recommended:

- **Association of Development Agencies in Bangladesh, NGO Affairs Bureau and the professional accounting institutes to work together to promote international standards of accounting, reporting and auditing in NGOs.**

[11] Prime Minister's Office (1993) *Working Procedure for Foreign and Foreign Assisted Bangladeshi Non-Government Voluntary Organisations,* and interview with the Director General of the Bureau.
[12] World Bank (2000h), pp. 27-30.
[13] CGAP (1998) *External Audits of Microfinance Institutions: A Handbook.* Technical Tool Series 3, p.7.

9. Private Sector Accountants and Auditors

9. Private Sector Accountants and Auditors

The Structure of the Profession

Two leading professional associations dominate the accounting/auditing profession. The Institute of Chartered Accountants of Bangladesh (ICAB) was established in 1973 by a Presidential Order. The Institute of Cost and Management Accountants of Bangladesh (ICMAB) was constituted by an Ordinance of 1977. Both bodies fall under the purview of the Ministry of Commerce, and are in receipt of annual government grants and occasional ADP project funding.

For a country having a population of 130 million, and 42,000 companies, the number of professional accountants is extremely low. At June 1999 there were less than a thousand working in Bangladesh, or about 8 per million of population, compared with India's 98 per million and the UK's 4,611 per million.[1]

The supply of accountants is low, partly for lack of adequate training facilities and lack of support for trainees from poor families,[2] but also because of low demand for accountancy services. The industrial and finance sectors, which are accountant-intensive, are still relatively small. Banks tend to use MBAs rather than professional accountants for financial analysis of projects (where this is done at all). More significantly, there is little appreciation of the value added by competent audit, and audit fees are correspondingly low. In the whole history of Bangladesh there has never been legal action against an auditor for professional negligence. This reflects low expectations and a lack of understanding of the significance of audit rather than high technical and ethical standards of auditors. The company law is considerably in advance of public understanding.

There is no accounting manpower study for the country, projecting the future demand and supply of accountants for accounting, auditing (public practice), teaching and consultancy functions. Neither the ICAB nor the ICMAB has a written strategic plan, but a few members of the respective Councils are seriously considering future needs in a globalized and Internet world, such as regional harmonization of standards and mutual recognition, and how their institutions should be preparing themselves. The ICAB is working on a strategic plan for raising accounting and auditing standards.

Training and Professional Development

Both the ICAB and ICMAB emphasize the maintenance of quality. Each institute has graduate entry and has recently revised its examination syllabus to equip trainees with managerial skills as well as technical competence. Post-qualification continuing education has become mandatory. There is a strong emphasis on information technology and English language training. The institutes are proud of the integrity of their examination and accreditation processes. Admission to membership requires also minimum periods (3-4 years) of practical training in an acceptable office.[3, 4] The number of registered trainees is very high (ICAB 7,000; ICMAB 13,000

---

[1] IFAC database on accredited member-bodies, summarized in Bennett (2000).
[2] Trainees get insufficient salaries to live on while under training. This effectively limits entry to students from middle class families.
[3] The ICAB does not at present allow articled clerks to get their practical training in the C&AG Office.

including an additional 2,051 in 1999) but the drop out rate is also high: only about 30-35 successfully complete the examinations each year.[5] One reason is that trainees come usually from a university education in Bengali whereas the medium of accountancy training and examination is English, which dominates the commercial sector. The recruitment and training arrangements do not appear to be attracting and holding sufficient numbers of young people with the potential to qualify. The entry points and training structure need to be re-examined.

Only 7% of trainees are women (ICAB 3%, ICMAB 10%), and the number who succeed and continue in the profession is miniscule. The ICAB has made small steps towards expanding opportunities for women, such as allowing practicing accountants who have reached the limit of 12 trainees to take one more if she is a woman.

There is little or no private sector provision of training. Training is done entirely by the two institutes. The ICMAB and ICAB are each planning an Academic Complex. The ICAB is getting World Bank assistance with the modernization of its Computer Training Center and the establishment of an English Learning Center. ICAB training materials date from UNDP project assistance in 1982/83 and should be revised and updated.

All education and training has so far been oriented to the full professional qualification. There is not yet any sub-professional qualification, such as Accounting Technician. Professional accountants are very few and their productivity would be higher if they had lower-level technicians to whom routine work could be delegated. The introduction of an Accounting Technician qualification, as in UK, Sri Lanka, etc. would provide a recognized accreditation, clearly distinct from the CA and CMA, which would appeal to those who have an aptitude for accounting and auditing work, but not necessarily the educational background or the perseverance to go all the way. Also it would reduce the dropout rate in the professional examinations by streaming entrants to the profession. The experience of Sri Lanka may be a useful guide (see box).

Box 7

Association of Accounting Technicians of Sri Lanka - AAT(SL)

In 1986, an ADB report highlighted the shortage of accounting and audit personnel at middle level in both the public and private sectors and estimated that the country would need 12,000 accounting technicians by the year 2000. Thus, in 1987, the AAT(SL) was established on the initiative of the Institute of Chartered Accountants of Sri Lanka (ICASL) according to the guidelines issued by IFAC, the Confederation of Asia and Pacific Accountants, and the AAT of UK.

So far, the AAT(SL) has been running as a company limited by guarantee, but it is seeking legislation to provide a sounder legal constitution. The Association has been supported by the ADB. It is run by a Governing Council comprising 8 nominees of the ICASL, 2 Government nominees and 5 elected by the members. At September 2000 there were 2,714 members and over 4,000 registered students. The AAT(SL) runs training courses and its own examinations and is self-financing. Most members go on to professional-level examinations.

---

[4] For a CA to offer services as an auditor, an additional two years of experience are required and a practising licence from the ICAB.

[5] The average of the last three years has been 13 chartered accountants and 18 management accountants per annum.

Compliance with Standards and Professional Discipline

Recent surveys of compliance of listed companies with the requirements of the Companies Act, SEC Rules and BAS show general compliance with the minimum letter of the law (with some major exceptions in group accounts, foreign exchange effects, leasing and earnings per share), but poor understanding of the spirit of disclosure. Two particular omissions in directors' reports are post-balance sheet events and future prospects (Imam 1999, World Bank 2000c). On the audit side, there have been allegations of corporate misreporting and fraud that should have been discovered and reported by the auditors. A clean audit certificate does not assure the National Board of Revenue that statements are a reliable basis for tax assessments. The ICAB has a Code of Ethics for its members and an Investigation and Disciplinary Committee that can investigate allegations against them, but this self-regulation so far has been inadequate and ineffective. The ICMAB is planning to introduce a Code of Ethics and its own disciplinary machinery, and will need to change its bylaws. At present, however, there is virtually no monitoring of technical and ethical standards of members. The World Bank-IDF grant to ICAB covers a survey of published accounts, preparation of case studies and training in the application of IAS and ISA.

Professional accountants, in their various roles as accountants, internal auditors and external auditors, are the eyes and ears of accountability. They are in the best position to know when managers try to defraud the organization or others outside the organization, since they guard the gateway to all money transactions by the organization. When accountants are members of a professional body with an ethical code, accounting becomes a tool of good economic governance and provides much of the ethical guidance by which laws and regulations are followed. The chartered accountants have a code of ethics and the management accountants are in the process of preparing theirs. The tough part is ensuring that members understand their importance and comply.

Recommendations are as follows:

- **Professional institutes to prepare strategic plans to expand the output of professional accountants and auditors without sacrificing quality.**

- **Set up a sub-professional accounting qualification.**

- **ICMAB to introduce a code of ethics, and both professional institutes to enforce their codes strictly.**

10. Next Steps

This assessment is of a country that is struggling to build open, democratic and transparent institutions on a legacy of colonial rule and military dictatorships. Enormous gains have been made in the institutionalization of democracy, particularly since 1991. But this is only ten years. It is not surprising that financial management is still extremely weak and that there are tremendous 'gaps' when accountability is compared against international standards. Nevertheless, reform starts with an acknowledgement of these weaknesses and a willingness to look ahead and review options and strategies for the continued development of standards. At present, public resources, whether provided from domestic or external sources, are at very considerable risk of being used for purposes other than those for which they were intended. Without significant improvement in fiscal probity, the assessment will remain unfavorable. From a donor perspective, the move from individual project support to programmatic support requires sound and transparent financial management and procurement systems. These preconditions cannot be said to exist in Bangladesh at present.

The assessment has found that the gap between international standards and national standards is not as serious as the gap between national standards and national practices. Laws and regulations exist, but are not enforced. At present there are few visible sanctions for wrongdoing. As laws and regulations have not been enforced they have fallen into disuse and often been forgotten. This suggests that a program to raise accountability standards will need to be accompanied by widespread refresher training of public officers on the regulatory framework. It also suggests that the program will have to give priority to senior levels of public officer, since their behavior sets unofficial standards for lower-level officers. The changes will involve a phased, medium-term program of 5-10 years.

The prospects for such a program, as for any governance reform program, depend on the decisions and actions of the political-administrative directorate. Past experience shows that reform proposals often die at the top. Bangladesh has a relatively open society: public sector reforms are widely and frankly debated. Issues are put on the table and consensus is often reached at workshops and conferences of stakeholders. However, the debate is sterile: little or no action follows. There is a 'disconnect' between thought and action. The same recommendations are made repeatedly each year. Many of the recommendations in this report parallel the recommendations of the Public Administration Reforms Commission. The damning reports of the Public Accounts Committee and Committee on Public Undertakings are not acted on. It appears that there are insufficient incentives within the Government to change the status quo.

Some reforms have succeeded through consensus building and participation, such as the RIBEC family of projects. These reforms had to benefit *all* the stakeholders whose cooperation was needed, so their scope and impact have been limited and constrained by the unwillingness to change organizational structures which protect the interests of public sector officials (World Bank 2000h, p.85). There is a limit to how far purely 'technical' reforms can go without changing who controls what and stepping on toes and prejudicing perceived interests. The interests of the public are being sacrificed to the interests of a relatively small number of public officials.

A key recommendation, therefore, is to mobilize support for reform from all who would benefit from it, both within the Government and without. The outside stakeholders include citizen groups and advocacy organizations that represent them (including the media, the local chapter of Transparency International, academia and the Public Administration Reform

Commission), the business community and their associations, and the donor community. At present there is little or no continuing collaboration among these groups for the promotion of accountability and transparency. The demand for change is fragmented and ineffective. Nor is there any network of public officers who have an interest in restoring the reputation of their government, but who are individually powerless and unwilling to speak out against the current ethos. Though there are some officials who have made progress in an adverse environment, they are few and scattered. The proposal is to establish a continuing public forum of oversight agencies, civil society organizations and individuals for the enhancement of accountability, transparency and the rule of law. The initiative for this should be taken by the C&AG, whose audit directorates provide the main center of oversight of public funds management. Donor agencies should agree on joint support to the establishment and operations of the forum.

A second key recommendation for implementation is for greater transparency of public sector activities. The media, for instance, cannot function effectively as part of the accountability system unless public agencies issue regular performance and financial reports on their activities. These should be submitted regularly to Parliament and made available at the same time to the public both in print and on a web site.

Accountability and transparency are the handmaidens of democracy. The progress made over the past decade has neglected these dimensions. Concerted action is now urgently needed to improve the status of accountability and transparency in Bangladesh.

◇References

Ahmed, Birhanuddin (Convenor) (1990) Government Malpractices, Report of Committee

Bangladesh, Government of. Cabinet Division (1996) Rules of Business

Bangladesh, Government of. and UNDP (1997) Implementation Plan on Strengthening of the Parliament (being final report by the team leader of BGD/96/017, Dr Najma Chowdhury)

Bangladesh, Government of. Ministry of Finance (1999). "Feasibility Study on Defence Accounts." March, Internal Control Unit.

Bennett, Anthony. (2000). "The Role of Accounting in Good Governance." in Yassin El-Ayouty, ed., *Government Ethics and Law Enforcement: Toward Global Guidelines.* Ed. by. New York: Greenwood Publishing Group.

Chowdhury, Mhd. Muslim. (1999). "An Insight into the C&AG (Additional Functions) Act, 1974." in *Public Money and Management.* (Annual Journal of FIMA) (November).

Chowdhury, Rezauddin M. (1998). "Use and Abuse of Suspense Accounts: A Study." *Public Finance and Development,* (January-June): 90-102.

Chowdhury, Riazur Rahman. (1999). "Comptroller and Auditor General's Report: An Analysis." *Public Money and Management* (Annual Journal of FIMA) (November).

Comptroller and Auditor-General of Bangladesh. (1999). *Government Auditing Standards.* Dhaka.

Imam, Shahed. (1999). "Regulation and its compliance in Bangladesh." *The Cost and Management* (Journal of the ICMAB) (September-October).

International Management Consultants and S.F. Ahmed & Co. (1993) Reforms in Budgeting and Expenditure Control, Final Report

INTOSAI (1992) *Auditing Standards.* Available from INTOSAI website www.intosai.org

Iskander, Magdi R. and Nadereh Chamlou. (2000). *"Corporate Governance: A Framework for Implementation."* Washington: World Bank Group

Khan, M. Abu Sayed. (1996). "Public Sector Accounting and Financial Reporting Practices in Bangladesh." Doctoral thesis for Management Centre, University of Bradford, UK.

Khan, Zakir Ahmed. (1998). "Public Sector Financial Management System in the UK and USA: Lessons for Bangladesh." *Public Finance and Development.* (Jan-Jun): 60-89.

Kibria, Shah A.M.S. (2000). "The Budget Speech 2000-01." as reported in the Daily Star, June 9

Local Government Commission. (1997). "Strengthening of Local Government Institutions: Report"

McMurran, John and Mhd. Hassanul Abedin Khan. (1997). "The Management Accounting Function – an Essential Tool for Effective Financial Control in Government." *Public Finance and Development.* 2/1. (July-December).

Ministry of Commerce. (1997). "Cost Audit (Report) Rules." 1997.

Ministry of Finance, Finance Division. (1998a). *"Compilation of the General Financial Rules".*

_____. (1998b). *"Treasury Rules and Subsidiary Rules Made Thereunder."*

National Wages and Productivity Commission. (1998). Report.

Office of the Comptroller & Auditor General of Bangladesh. (1997). *"Annual Report."* Dhaka.

_____. (1998). *"Annual Report."* Dhaka.

Parry, Michael and Ferdous Khan. (1984). *"A Survey of Published Accounts in Bangladesh."* Dhaka: Institute of Chartered Accountants of Bangladesh and UN Department of Technical Cooperation for Development.

Public Administration Reform Commission. (2000). *"Public Administration for the 21st Century."* Report of the Public Administration Reform Commission. In 3 volumes, June.

Rabbani, A.K.M. Ghulam. (1998). "The Bangladesh general government sector and its sub-sectors." (October). See also *"Public Finance and Development."* (Jan-June 1998): 29-49.

Rahman, Masihur. (1996). "Formulation of National Budget." *Public Finance and Development.* 1/1, (July-December).

Rahman Rahman Huq. (1999a). "Financial and Operational Plan for City Corporations/Paurashavas: Kurigram Paurashava." (30 June).

_____. (1999b). "Financial and Operational Plan for City Corporations/Paurashavas: Rajshahi City Corporation." (12 July).

RIBEC. (2000a). "Way Forward for Financial Management Reforms in Bangladesh." first draft. (21 March).

_____. (2000b). Project Accounting Manual.

_____. (2000c). "Quality of Financial Information: Bank Reconciliation." (May).

RIBEC Project. (1993). "Technical Paper No. 2: The Budget System." Final report. (June).

_____. (1999b). "Food Accounts Study." First draft – External. (March).

_____. (1999c). "The Bangladesh Railway Authority Accounting Study." Second draft. (March).

_____. (1999d). "Feasibility Study on the Integration of Telegraph and Telephone Accounts with the Civil Accounts of the Government of Bangladesh." First draft – External. (May).

_____. (1999e). "Feasibility Study on Foreign Aid Accounting." First draft- external. (June).

_____. (1999f). "Project Accounting Manual." Draft. (October).

_____. (undated). "An Alternative Model of the Annual Financial Statement and Annual Budget of the Government of Bangladesh for the Year ended 30 June 1998".

RIBEC 2A Project. (1996). Accounts Code." Vols. 1 and 2 (bound together). (September).

_____. (1997a). Classification Chart. (March).

RIBEC 2B Project. (1997b). "Review of Future Priorities and Plans for Financial Management Reforms." Draft report. (March).

_____. (1997c). "Internal Audit Feasibility Study." Final Draft – External. (November).

_____. (1997d). "Consolidated Accounting System – the Quality and Flow of Financial Information." First draft – External. (November).

_____. (1997e). "Review of Audit Requirements and Wider Audit Issues Arising from the Implementation of Phase 2B." Final draft – External. (November).

_____. (1999a). "Feasibility Reports: Combining Revenue and Development Budget, Integrating of Development Plans to Development Budget; Future Role of Budget Committees in Line Ministries." First Draft – External. (January).

Sahgal, Vinod. (1999). "Financial Accountability in Bangladesh: A Governance Perspective".

Schacter, Mark. (2000). "When Accountability Fails: A Framework for Diagnosis and Action. Institute of Governance Policy Brief No. 9."

Soliman, Magdy Martinez and Kendra P. Collins. (2000). "Advisory Opinion on the Reform of the Rules of Procedure (GOB/UNDP Project on Strengthening Parliamentary Democracy BGD/97/003)." two volumes.

Standing Committee on Public Accounts. (1998). "Third Report of the Committee, Seventh Parliament." (November).

Transparency International, Bangladesh Chapter. (1997). "Survey of Households and Providers of Public Services."

UNDP. (2000). "CONTACT: Country Assessment in Accountability and Transparency." 2nd edition. (June 2000). New York: Management Development and Governance Division.

World Bank. (1996a). *Government That Works: Reforming the Public Sector.* Dhaka: The University Press.

_____. (1996b). *Bangladesh Public Expenditure Review.* Country Operations Division/Resident Mission. Dhaka.

_____. (1997a). *Bangladesh Public Expenditure Review: 1997 Update.* South Asia Region.

_____. (1997b). *Bangladesh Municipal Finance Management Study.* Infrastructure Operations Division, Country Department 1, South Asia Region, Washington DC. (May).

_____. (1998a). "Bangladesh: Strategy for Establishing a Sound and Competitive Banking Sector." 3 volumes, Finance and Private Sector Unit, South Asia Region. (May).

_____. (1998b). "Bangladesh: Country Profile of Financial Accountability." Resident Mission, Dhaka. (June).

_____. (1999a). "Bangladesh: Country Procurement Assessment Report." Volume I: Summary and Recommendations; Volume II: Findings and Analysis; Discussion Paper, Resident Mission, Dhaka.

_____. (1999b). *Project Financial Management Manual.* Exposure draft, Loan Department, Washington DC. February.

_____. (1999c). "Country Financial Accountability Assessment." Draft report by Loan Department, Washington DC. (December 17).

_____. (2000a). "Public Sector Modernization: Project Concept Document." Dhaka. (March 6).

_____. (2000b). "Budgeting, Accounting and Internal Control." Report prepared for World Bank, Dhaka. (May).

_____. (2000c). "Review of Accounting Profession and Education in Bangladesh." Report prepared for World Bank, Dhaka. (May).

_____. (2000d). "Parliamentary Control over Public Expenditure in Bangladesh: The Role of Committees." Report prepared for World Bank, Dhaka. (May).

_____. (2000e). "Financial Accountability of Local Government Institutions." Report prepared for World Bank, Dhaka. (May).

_____. (2000f). "Public Sector Auditing." report prepared for World Bank, Dhaka. (May).

_____. (2000g). "The Experience and Perceptions of Public Officials in Bangladesh." Dhaka. (May).

_____. (2000h). "Taming Leviathan: Reforming Governance in Bangladesh, An Institutional Review." Dhaka. (September, 2000).